Heart
of a
Champion

Other books in the Zonderkidz Biography Series:

Heart of a Champion

the
Dominique Dawes
Story

Kim Washburn

ZONDER**kidz**

ZONDERVAN.com/
AUTHORTRACKER
· follow your favorite authors

ZONDERKIDZ

Heart of a Champion
Copyright © 2012 by Kim Washburn

This title is also available as a Zondervan ebook.

Visit www.zondervan.com/ebooks

Requests for information should be addressed to:
Zonderkidz, 5300 Patterson Ave SE, Grand Rapids, Michigan 49530

ISBN: 978-0-310-72268-7

Cover design: Kris Nelson
Interior composition: Greg Johnson/TextbookPerfect

Printed in the United States

12 13 14 15 16 17 18 /DCI/ 22 21 20 19 18 17 16 15 14 13 12 11 10 9 8 7 6 5 4 3 2 1

For ABB, AVJ, and ALK

Gutsy girls who leave me laughing and inspired.

Table of Contents

Introduction

Thank you for reading about my journey in the sport of gymnastics. I pray that you are able to find your own "D-3" Determination Dedication Desire from my story.

Aspiring to Inspire!

Dominique Dawes
2000 96
92

Chapter 1

Success Under Pressure

"Success is a journey not a destination."

In less than a minute, she will attack her routine with the stature of a pixie, the power of a firework, and the flexibility of Elastigirl. But until she gets the signal, Dominique Dawes quietly stands at the edge of the spring floor, shouldering the pressure and clearing her thoughts.

The crowd buzzes in the arena and TV commentators list her accomplishments. But in her mind Dominique turns down the volume of all the distractions just like she turned down the volume when she watched gymnastics on TV at home.

She takes a breath and waits. She has been in this position before and she knows what she has to do. Although still a teenager, Dominique is by all accounts an experienced veteran.

For twelve years, she has trained to do tricks that defy gravity despite the weight of the situation. Still sometimes the physical gymnastics came easier than the mental ones. How does one simply set aside past setbacks and future goals, minor mistakes and big dreams?

The petite and powerful girl in the blue velvet leotard sees her signal. Without blinking Dominique steps inside the corner of the mat, takes another breath, and focuses. The music sweeps through the speakers.

Dominique takes two hard-charging steps, then launches into the air like on springs. When she lands in the opposite corner, she doesn't stop or even pause before propelling herself in the *opposite* direction. With dizzying speed she successfully completes no less than eleven tricks on one supersonic up-and-back tumbling pass.

The roar of the crowd overtakes the music but Dominique has practiced so many hours, she doesn't miss a beat. With pointed toes, straight legs, perfect posture, and jumps that are higher than a grown man's head, she performs her routine with precision and power. Timing her last movement with the last note, the crowd cheers enthusiastically. She raises her arms with the posture of a champion.

Back on the side of her mat, Dominique meets her coach — the dedicated instructor and positive guide whose face she has looked up to since her first somersault. Dominique accepts the congratulations, smiles briefly, listens to the feedback, and waits for the score.

Would her performance be enough to accomplish

Doug Pensinger/ALLSPORT/Getty Images

Dominique tumbles through the floor exercise into first place overall in the 1994 Senior Women's US National Gymnastics Championships in Nashville, Tennessee.

something that hasn't been done in twenty-five years? She waits for the judges.

Dominique had been in a gym for a decade, making the most of the gifts God had given her. Although her strong muscles masked a fragile self-esteem, she persevered through difficulties and dedicated her life to rare, elite competition. Her incredible accomplishments belied a young girl under significant pressure to be perfect—because even if God doesn't require perfection, the international judges do.

Slow minutes pass and the score is posted. She looks at the three small numbers, one step toward a gigantic achievement: Dominique wins the all-around portion of the competition—and goes on to win each of the four individual events as well. By the end of the meet, she is the first gymnast in twenty-five years to "sweep the board."

The significant accomplishment is one in a long line. By age 23 Dominique won more national championship medals than any other athlete—boy or girl—since 1963, became the only American to medal in an unprecedented three Olympics, was the first African-American to win an Olympic individual medal as well as win Olympic gold with her artistic gymnastic team, was the first African-American national champion.

But this story is getting ahead of itself. This account is far more than a long list of unique accomplishments and accolades. It's a rolling, twisting journey of passion, challenge, inspiration, heartbreak, humility, and life lessons. It didn't begin with a score from a judge. And it certainly doesn't end there.

Chapter 2

The Blessings That Brought Her Here

"There was always an emphasis on a strong foundation."

This story really starts in 1976. The summer Olympic Games of the XXI Olympiad were held in Montreal, Canada, where the gymnastic competition was dominated by Eastern European teams and a fourteen-year-old Romanian named Nadia Comãneci. That year no female gymnast from the United States won a medal.

Five hundred miles away in Silver Spring, Maryland, a little girl with a big Olympic future was born. Dominique Margaux Dawes was the second daughter of Don and Loretta. A coordinated ball of energy, she kept everyone on their toes and did her best to keep up with her four-year-old big sister, Danielle.

Dad was dedicated to the family business he inherited

from his father. Often up at three in the morning and back at eight in the evening, he worked hard to earn a living. Mom worked at home keeping the financial books for the business. Meanwhile the sisters bounced around the furniture, spent time with close cousins, and helped around the house as they got older.

The girls had their own rooms until Dominique was six, when her brother, Don Jr., was born. Then the sisters started sharing a room and a bunk bed. "I always stayed at the bottom because I was a very active sleeper," Dominique recalled, "especially after I started gymnastics because your body ends up twitching and you end up moving a lot more. So I was always on the bottom bunk and never excited about that. I always wanted to sneak up to the top bunk."[1]

If she wasn't sleeping, Dominique was moving. Possessing plenty of energy, she could go for hours, even after a day at school. So Mrs. Dawes looked for an outlet. "My parents put me in a sport," Dominique said. "They did what all parents do—they tried to channel their child's energy in a positive way."[2]

If she could spring around the house, then why not spring around a gym? They signed Danielle and Dominique up for a tumbling class that ended up being cancelled. ("My mom *claims* I was devastated," Dominique smiled.) At the same time, they happened to hear about another gym called Hill's Angels. Why not? At least *that* class wasn't cancelled. So Dominique signed up and started working with coach Kelli Hill.

In the most plain, unassuming way, her parents were

simply doing a logical thing by finding their little girl a positive diversion. Looking back, it's hard not to see a divine plan that led to the coach who Dominique would have for nearly two decades.

"My mother had no interest in sports. She hates sweating. And my dad knew nothing about gymnastics, and it [seemed] really by chance that my sister and I ended up signing up. I really do think it was definitely God's hands that made this happen. I have no other gift in any other sport. I've tried other things—been horrible. The Lord blessed me with these talents and opened that door for me to flourish in gymnastics."

When Dominique first started, it wasn't obvious yet that God had gifted her with ability and passion for gymnastics. And it wasn't obvious yet that through the sport, she would touch countless lives.

But there we go again, jumping ahead.

Her new gym offered more than just somersaults on a mat. There Dominique learned skills on four different disciplines—floor exercise, uneven bars, balance beam, and vault. Each apparatus called for flexibility, balance, power, fearlessness, coordination, and physical toughness. Dominique did very well. "If you start young, it's not so hard, not so fearful," Dominique proposed. "But yes, if you start older, even ten years old, it becomes a lot harder to learn these tricks."[3]

Since Dominique was six, the tricks came well with practice. She liked it and she was good at it. God had blessed her individually. Now what would she do with the blessings?

Of the thousands of American girls who annually start kindergym, tumbling, or gymnastics at a young age, only a fraction end up competing seriously. Less than a hundred colleges around the United States keep less than twenty athletes on their rosters.[4] Less than fifteen girls total represent the United States on the junior national team, twenty on the senior national team. Only seven girls across the entire country make the Olympic team every four years.

It is an exclusive group that possesses the many skills to compete. Physically, real contenders must have extraordinary fitness, toughness, strength, courage, and coordination. Mentally, they must possess unusual focus, discipline, tenacity, and desire to pursue long-term goals in the face of short-term distractions.

Furthermore, circumstances have to be right. The right coach and training facilities have to be nearby. The athlete also has to be free from injury during the constant stress on her body. Injuries, growth spurts, and limitations that come with age can undercut even the most elite competitor.

On top of it all, timing plays an essential role. For example, Olympic opportunities come only two times in a decade. An otherwise qualified gymnast who misses the age requirements by a couple of months is out of luck. For the gymnast, the window of opportunity is uniquely short. Past her prime in her early twenties, her best chance to compete comes during busy school years.

So when everything comes together, the "stars align"

and lightning strikes and God ordains, an elite gymnast is made.

Dominique was one of the rare ones who had been blessed with physical attributes, uncommon discipline, good health, and favorable circumstances. Plus, she just liked being in the gym. "I felt very much at home," she admitted. "It was an environment where I felt very comfortable. I really just felt like I belonged."[5]

In the gym she fit in perfectly for the same things that made her stand out at school. Teased for being the smallest or the squeakiest or the one with the most muscles, Dominique was reserved. "I found myself hiding in my shell in hopes that no one would notice me."[6]

A lot of girls dream of competing on the grand international stage of the Olympics. But with her gifts along with hard work and countless hours of practice, Dominique could actually make her dream a reality.

While in elementary school, Dominique trained every afternoon. A few times a week, she also practiced *before* school. On those mornings, she got up before the sun at four forty-five to leave the house by five thirty.

At six in the morning, the gym was empty, except for Dominique, Coach Kelli, and Kelli's infant son bundled in blankets on the floor. "My coach's gym really didn't have great heat, so I remember in the winter going, and it would be so cold that you could see your breath," smiled Dominique. "I would run around to warm up, and she would go to McDonald's to get hot chocolate for me."[7]

After practicing for two hours, her coach took her to school. When the final bell rang at three, Dominique ran home—literally *ran* the entire mile. "And it was up a hill for about a quarter of a mile!" she remembered. At home she had time to watch half of one cartoon before leaving for the afternoon practice which lasted from four until nine.[8]

Waking up every day before dawn was hard enough on the determined girl with the big dreams, but it also affected the rest of her family. Sometimes her mom, tired from juggling work and three kids, was just too exhausted to get up. On those occasions, Dominique called her coach devastated that she was missing training and crying that her mom didn't share her intensity. "This dream doesn't mean anything to her!" she would say before her coach would calm her down. Later she admitted that she understood. "When I sit back and think about it, it was a lot on my parents."[9]

Eventually Coach Kelli invited Dominique to stay at her house near the gym on the nights before morning practice. Then those mornings only coach and athlete would have to get up to get to the gym.

Before her age hit double digits, Dominique was dutifully practicing her fundamentals and proper technique. She stretched her limbs, pointed her toes, lengthened her line, learned how to land, learned how to fall, jumped higher, and whipped faster. She balanced on a four-inch wide beam; she swung around a bar; she flew over a pommel horse; she danced on a bare spring floor. And she flipped over everything. She landed in foam pits and soft mats. She shook off sprains and bruises. And she reached for perfect form in the biggest moves and the smallest details.

"Since the day I first tumbled in the gym, there was always an emphasis on building a strong foundation and improving my fundamentals," Dominique explained. "It began with proper form and presentation, then cardio and flexibility work, followed by strength and core conditioning, and finally ending with basic tumbling and dance elements."[10]

By age ten Dominique was travelling to U.S. championship events to compete in elite competition at the junior level.[11]

As she practiced the fundamentals, techniques, and physical tricks, she also worked on the demanding mental aspect. So Dominique sharpened necessary focus and developed the self-assurance it takes to perform under pressure. She realized she wasn't going to stand on an Olympic podium by her twelfth birthday, so she set little goals to help her achieve longer-term objectives.

It would take years. So she came up with a way to stay focused throughout the long journey of hard work, long hours, high scores, and low marks. Eleven-year-old Dominique Dawes created a personal motto, "D – 3: Determination, dedication, and desire" were the three Ds that she knew were key ingredients for her specific goal.

When pressure and distraction threatened to derail her efforts, D – 3 kept Dominique focused and inspired, especially to keep striving for the Olympics. "I used to spray this saying with shaving cream on this huge mirror that I had in my bedroom," Dominique admits. "My parents hated it," she confessed with a smile.[12]

But for Dominique, the motto helped. *D–3* kept her focused on the positive instead of the negative. *D–3* meant using a stumble as a stepping stone. Instead of focusing on what she was giving up or what went wrong at practice, *D–3* kept her focused on the journey of her achievements.

The goal was the podium but her true success in gymnastics remained in daily practice, positive attitude, perseverance. Her success would happen over time, not just when she reached one goal. *D–3* would keep her on the path.

After spending half of her life in the gym, Dominique took a trip halfway around the globe to Australia in her first international meet, the Konica Grand Prix. Although she was the youngest competitor, Dominique looked every bit the pro. With glitter in her hair, she walked primly to the middle of the twelve-by-twelve spring floor and struck a pose to await the cue in the music.

The announcer noted her presence: "She's a real powerhouse. And we'll see that in this first tumbling section: full-twisting, double-back somersault." Despite lofty amplitude, she landed it with confident force. "I don't believe she's only twelve," the announcer continued. "We can see why she's ranked one of the best juniors in the United States."[13]

On the last tumbling pass, Dominique landed on her feet—and a little bit on her head at the same time. Without missing a beat, she stood up and continued. She finished with her confident end pose and strode off the mat. "That's character," the commentator pointed out. "A strong finish."[14]

Set apart by her young age, excellent execution, and strong character, Dominique also stood apart because of her race. "Gymnastics is a sport dominated by Caucasians," she admitted, "but that statistic did not affect my hope and dream of someday becoming an Olympic gold medalist."[15] *D–3*—determination, dedication, desire—wouldn't allow the distraction.

The next year, Dominique earned third in the all-around junior division at the U.S. National Championships.[16] That is, the combined score for her performances on the beam, vault, floor, and bars, earned her a spot on the podium.

She continued to progress, continued to place high in competition, continued to set goals. "I feel like I would like to turn on the crowd, not the crowd turn on me," said fifteen-year-old Dominique. "I'd like to just keep smiling and get them into my routine and for them to feel the enthusiasm that I'm feeling at the same time."[17]

Girls who liked watching her powerful tricks and knew of her years of dedication wrote fan mail to the young gymnast. Early in her career she started to realize how she could impact others not just with her performance and perseverance, but by how she acted, by how she treated others, even by how she struggled.

"I really think that God placed me in the gymnastics arena because that was my passion," she said, "but my purpose is to inspire people with that passion."[18]

Chapter 3

What Teamwork Can Do

"You have to surround yourself with positive people."

"My dream is to be on the 1992 Olympic team in Barcelona," fifteen-year-old Dominique said. "And I'd also like to stay in the sport and hopefully get a college scholarship. And then if I'm strong and healthy and able to do gymnastics at a really good caliber, I'd like to go for [the Olympics] in '96."[19]

The dreams were huge, but the window of opportunity was small. So armed with dedication, determination and drive, Dominique had to go for it. Five days a week she was at the gym to train before anyone her age had even turned off their alarm for school. Because she was working out twice a day every day, Dominique stayed with her coach's family and went to high school near the gym. "Accepting the fact that their daughter might have to move away was one thing they (her parents) agreed to," Dominique admitted.[20] It was a sacrifice for everyone but it made a busy schedule more manageable.

Before school, coach and athlete headed to the gym from six to eight for training. Then Dominique went to her new high school for four classes, then went back to the gym for five more hours of stretching, ballet, and practice.[21]

To stay in the kind of shape gymnastics required meant year-round training. "Kelli always joked that you get Christmas Eve [*evening*] off but you work out in the morning," Dominique remembered. "We never thought that was too funny," she smiled.[22]

In truth, though, nobody had to convince Dominique to go to the gym. The longest time she'd been away was a weeklong summer vacation when she was about ten. "I remember thinking, *Oh, this is so much fun! I'll eat whatever I want! I'll lay out at the beach!* And then I came back to practice after the vacation and could do *nothing*. For a gymnast, when you put on a couple pounds it makes a huge difference. And I really forgot how to do a lot of my gymnastics, like it was a *struggle*. And after that experience Kelli said, 'No more vacations for you!'" Dominique laughed.[23]

"She was a really tough coach," Dominique continued, "but honestly I'm very thankful because it taught me the importance of work ethic, being committed to something, and sacrificing things."[24]

With all that time spent together, Kelli Hill became

more than a coach to Dominique. She was a mentor, role model, and second mom. Years later, Dominique reflected on their relationship. "I wouldn't be where I am without her support and guidance," Dominique said. "I didn't get here on my own. In my eighteen years in the sport, she did a very good job protecting me from everything that was going on outside of gymnastics. She made me focus on the things I had control of and everything else was just put aside in a stack—everything from how the judges felt about me to the temperature of the gym. She was very big on instilling that lesson."[25]

For Dominique it left a lasting impression about the company one keeps. "For you to be a positive person, remember you have to surround yourself with positive people," she said. "Don't hang with negative people. Don't hang with people who are going to bring you down."[26]

Dominique relied on her coach. And each knew their role to play, Dominique as dedicated athlete, and Kelli Hill as motivator and guide. "I never believed I was that disciplined as a child. I just did what I loved. To this day Kelli says, 'You have the most drive and determination that I've seen. I always just wanted to be there.'"

Crediting her coach, Dominique said, "I truly believe that if I didn't have her tough, tough love, I wouldn't have made it on any Olympic team." She admitted that her coach simply would not allow her "to be content with a sixty or seventy percent effort, and would not allow [her] to talk [herself] out of something."[27]

Every day her goal of the Olympics got closer. And every day she practiced, refined technique, made adjustments, worked on mental toughness, focused on *D–3*. It was a long continual process. "Coach always told me success is a journey, not a destination."[28] They were on the journey together.

After several months of living with her coach and making the most of her daily routine, Dominique was getting attention on gymnastics' worldwide stage. At the Dodge Challenge, she was the leader after three rotations. She needed a 9.410 on the floor exercise to win.

The picture of calm, the eighty-pound sophomore strode to the corner of the mat and waited for her cue. When the spirited music ramped up, the crowd anticipated speed, power, and amplitude. Dominique delivered, and went even further by delighting everyone with her rare up-and-back tumbling pass. With the benefit of slow-motion replay, the announcers noticed something the audience couldn't appreciate at full speed. At the beginning of her second pass, Dominique's foot slid just a little so she didn't get the push she needed.

"She over-rotated that front [flip] and her feet kind of slipped out from under her," explained the announcer. "Normally she does only two back handsprings. Here she added a third so she could get enough momentum to do the double back [somersault]. That is important in terms of her ability as a competitor to be able to think that fast."[29]

The crowd came to its feet for the four-foot, nine-inch fifteen-year-old. The judges approved, too, with a perfect 10.0.

At the U.S. Nationals that year, she showed her ability on a different apparatus by placing first on the bars. She pulled off a daring dismount that added a twist no one else was attempting.[30]

With good performances on each event at the Olympic trials, Dominique placed fourth in the all-around competition. Just five years after her first meet, she became one of the first African-American women to qualify for the U.S. Olympic gymnastics team.[31]

Her plans were no longer confined to a dream. Dominique was going to the Olympics to represent the United States.

The Games of the XXV Olympiad were held in July in Barcelona, the second largest city in Spain. The women's team skipped the opening ceremonies at the historic Estadi Olímpic Lluís Companys and focused on its goal of getting to the podium.

Artistic gymnastics drew large crowds to the new, sleek arena Palau Sant Jordi, where the team competition was held over two days. During the first round, five gymnasts compete on each of the four events. The top four scores are used to determine what teams advance to the team finals. During the second round, three gymnasts compete on each event, all three scores count, and the scores determine the medals.[32]

Dominique helped advance her team with ninety nail-biting seconds on the four-inch-wide, four-foot-high balance beam. Although it's impossible to play it *safe* on this apparatus, she went a step further with a bold, new

Dominique does her floor exercise during the 1992 Olympic Games in Barcelona, Spain.

Bob Martin/Getty Images

move—back handspring to three layout step-outs—and a difficult dismount which she landed expertly.

On the floor exercise she wowed the crowd with her up-and-back tumbling pass that she completed in practically less time than it takes to read each consecutive element aloud—round off/whip back/whip back/back handspring/double full/punch front somersault step up/round off/back handspring/back handspring/back handspring/double tuck. The spectators couldn't suppress their excitement.

"I couldn't hear my floor music after that tumbling pass," she said. "The crowd [was] cheering so loud; I just [had] to dance to their cheers. It was an amazing feeling."[33] Her score of 9.925 tied with teammate Kim Zmeskal for the highest score for the American team on floor.

Staggeringly, 192 million people tuned in as Dominique and her teammates stood on the podium and proudly wore the medal they earned for their performance as a team.[34] With beautiful bronze hanging from their necks, she and teammate Betty Okino became the first African-American females to win an Olympic gymnastics medal. With it they set a significant precedent in a sport that had historically done little to encourage multinationality participation in a country that values its history as a melting pot of cultures.

Dominique had battled painful tendinitis in both of her ankles and Osgood-Schlatter syndrome in her knees. She had endured emotional stress as she practiced and performed for countless hours over the years. She had exercised dedication, determination, and drive. Here she stood with a medal around her neck, one of seven elite athletes in the best, most visible gymnastic competition in the world.

Dominique knew it was a momentous achievement for herself, for young girls looking up to her, and for her country. What she didn't realize was that this was just the beginning.

Chapter 4

Nothing Less Than Perfect

"You want to at least try."

After competing for the team in the Olympics, Dominique used the next year to break out as an individual competitor. At World trials, she placed fourth on beam, second on bars, second on floor, and first on vault.

At the 1993 World Championships, Dominique joined competitors from fifty-seven nations in Birmingham, England. This was the first Worlds to have only two gymnasts per nation instead of three. Dominique was one of these top two gymnasts.

After three events in the all-around competition, Dominique led the field. The final apparatus was the vault, her gold event at the World trials. The scores of two vaults would be averaged, so both scores count, leaving zero room for error.

There's nothing easy about the Yurchenko-style of vault that includes a roundoff onto the springboard and a back handspring onto the horse. On top of that entry, the "one-and-a-half twisting layout Yurchenko" lands forward so the gymnast can't spot the mat before her feet land. The blind landing makes it especially difficult. For Dominique this vault was easier than the "Yurchenko double full," even though it was harder to land.

Dominique lined up on the runway, ran at full speed to the pommel horse, did a round-off onto the springboard, a back handspring onto the horse, a one and a half twisting layout, and a solid blind landing.

As she walked back for her second vault, she knew where she stood. She had been at the top of the leader board before. But her experience didn't ease the pressure. All of the training, practice, discipline came down to this one shot at the vault — five seconds, one landing.

Just like the first successful vault, Dominique ran full out. Good speed, nice height, perfect position in the air. But the last thing the judges saw was a fault on the landing. Dominique felt herself slip on the landing and felt her medal chances slip away.

Dominique's professional mask slipped away too. Feeling the weight of the disappointment, she couldn't hold in the tears as the judges worked on a score. But her coach Kelli Hill insisted the young gymnast be proud of her performance. "When did you ever think you would be in that position?" she asked. "You have to be happy with yourself. Come on. Be happy. Stand up and wave."

Chris Cole/Getty Images

Dominique cries after she loses her chance at a medal during
the 1993 World Gymnastics Championships. While suffering a
disappointing loss such as this, Dominique continued to believe in
herself and pushed through the obstacles to accomplish her goals.

Dominique listened, stood up, and waved to the
crowd. In sincere appreciation for her accomplishments
and her courage, the crowd also stood—and cheered.

After watching the competition, Dwight Normile,
editor of *International Gymnast* magazine, said this: "All
she had to do was land both vaults, and she would have
won at least a bronze medal. But she went for a more

difficult vault both times, fell on the second one and finished fourth. Still, people respected that she went for it, that she took the risk to get the reward."[35]

"You never want to be considered a quitter in life," Dominique said as she thought about taking an easier road. "You want to at least *try*."[36]

Regardless of the results, Dominique had to put it behind her. The all-around competition was over, but the individual event finals had yet to be determined. There was a lot more tumbling to do.

Within days Dominique went from disappointment to accomplishment. Her routine on the uneven bars earned her a silver medal. And her performance on the beam earned her another one. Her silvers meant even more than second place; they exemplified resilience and perseverance.

"There were many times that I wanted to quit [gymnastics]," Dominique admitted. "The physical stuff is not hard. It's the mental aspect — constantly getting yourself to believe in yourself and know that you can push through these obstacles."[37]

Every day Dominique had to push through mental and physical obstacles in pursuit of perfection. Because exacting judgments were inherent to the sport, an *excellent* score was not good enough. Only a *perfect* score satisfied. "In the gymnastic environment, you're always striving for that perfect ten. It very much molds you into a perfectionist," she noticed. "You start to believe that nothing is good enough unless it's perfect. That carried over throughout my childhood."[38]

Chris Cole/ALLSPORT/Getty Images

Dominique stretches out her hands towards the top bar as she performs a routine on the uneven bars at the 1993 World Gymnastics Championships. She ended up winning the silver medal in this event.

"As a child and teenager training nearly forty hours a week to qualify for the Olympics, I quickly developed a desire to please others," she admitted. "When you spend the majority of your childhood surrounded by an audience, you tend to seek applause. I vividly remember feeling disappointment if I did not live up to other people's expectations; and when I fell short of a goal, I would internalize it as a personal flaw. I also dealt with a painful feeling of unworthiness, which affected me not only in the athletic arena but also in my school and home environments."[39]

From the outside, all of Dominique's success at the gym and in the classroom looked enviable. But it came at a cost. Her pursuit of perfection not only proved elusive but ultimately corroded her contentment with anything less. She had to find a way to listen to the constructive criticism in order to polish her performance in the gym—but not take it further than that.

A few months after the World Championships, Dominique went to Salt Lake City to compete in the 1993 U.S. Nationals where she unveiled an outstanding performance on balance beam. This is how the announcer saw it: "I talked about the tremendous difficulty this young lady has in her beam routine. And at this point she is getting set, focused for one of the most difficult dismount sequences done in the world. Watch this: two flip-flops to a full-twisting double somersault. . . . She just rocks the landing!" Her performance earned her a gold medal for beam.

She also took home the silver in the all-around.

And the gold on vault.

Chapter 5

Breakthrough and Clean Sweep

"She didn't give me advice. She showed me compassion."

The World Championships in Brisbane, Australia, had a slightly different format in 1994. The gymnasts competed for the individual all-around and events only. The team event came later in the year.[40]

Dominique focused on the narrow beam for ninety eternal seconds of balance and control and breathtaking tricks. "Ultimate test of concentration," observed the analyst while he watched her routine. "Increased difficulty from her. Three somersaults in a row and plenty of confidence to go with them. Very difficult forward somersault. She's certainly looking very confident and poised. And the dismount—two flips into full-twisting double back—you won't see anything more difficult than that. Dominique Dawes setting a very high standard."[41]

Similarly she set a very high standard on the next two events and led the intense competition going into the final apparatus, the vault. Like the previous year, in order to take home a medal she simply had to complete it cleanly, like she knew she could.

She stood before the pommel horse and tried to clear her memory of last year's disappointment. Her body knew what to do—how to do tricks that looked like she was on the moon where there was no gravity. Her mind had to get out of the way.

The audience held its breath and watched the leader sprint down the runway and hurtle her straight body over the horse. She landed with power but overrotated. Propelled forward by the momentum, she somersaulted out the landing.

After standing and raising her arms for her pose to the judges, Dominique turned and walked back for her second vault. Although her face betrayed no break in emotion, she knew her medal chance was gone.

Standing composed at the end of the runway, Dominique waited for her disappointing score, a 9.250, and struggled to focus on what was in *front* of her. The commentator watched, saying, "She's got to pull herself together and give an account of herself. Concentration and maturity are the test for her." Without another word, he watched her complete the second vault. "And this time she got it right," he said approvingly. "The second vault so much improved on the first, but to no avail."

Like the previous year, Dominique fell on the landing, fell in the standings, and fell in her confidence. After her final pose and feat of concentration, the disappointment bubbled up. Even a word from her coach couldn't overcome the emotion of the setback. As the camera focused in on her face and flashed her score, Dominique packed her gym bag and got ready to go home.

If success was a journey, not a destination, then regardless of what happened in the meet she had to keep training. Medal around her neck or not, her journey continued. Gold, silver, bronze — or not — there were always things to work on, always things to learn.

Surprisingly what she learned next had nothing to do with the technique for the vault.

Her coach always encouraged Dominique to like who she was regardless of a score,[42] but Dominique's self-assurance suffered if her performance did. "I wasn't believing in myself," she admitted.[43]

The perfectionist athlete was suffering a crisis of confidence. "I was struggling for over a month each and every day of practice leading up the nationals," she remembered. "I couldn't stay on the balance beam to save my life. My consistency and confidence were failing. I am not sure if it was the pressure of the sport getting to me, but whatever it was, it made it difficult to stay focused on my goals."[44]

Then she heard some truth that lightened the weight on her shoulders.

"One day after practice, Mrs. Norman, a parent of

a teammate, took me aside and said the kindest words to me. She didn't add pressure or give me advice; she showed me compassion.[45] She came up to me and she said, 'You know what? We don't care if you come in last place. We don't care if you blow the meet. We don't love you for your gymnastics, we love you for you, for who you are and the way you treat people.'[46] To this day, her words still resonate in my head and inspire me to stay focused whenever times get tough. I learned then that saying the right words, at the right time, can lift someone's spirit. I aspire to offer those same kind words to those that I come in contact with.'[47]

Until this gentle moment, this idea had eluded Dominique. For years everything she did was measured and judged. Shackled by the fear of failure, she had lost the joy of the journey. But now, with this gesture, perspective, and insight, Dominique found some freedom, and with it more joy and confidence.

"Her saying that meant a lot to me because it let me know that it's not just about Dominique Dawes, the gymnast. It's about the way that I present myself and the way that I am...I guess, personable, and the way I treat others. And that people won't love you for your sport. They love you for the person that you are.'[48]

It was one of the most important steps in her journey. The words and sentiment would stay with her forever.

In August Dominique flew south to Nashville, Tennessee, for the U.S. National Championships. Her first event was the vault, where she planned the same one-and-a-half twisting Yurchenko that gave her trou-

Robert Reichert/Time Life Pictures/Getty Images

A portrait of Dominique at age 17.

ble at Worlds. In the moments it takes to count to five, Dominique would know if she was still in the medal hunt.

She went for it—and nailed it. The effort and execution earned her a gold in the event.[49]

In the event finals for the uneven bars, Dominique impressed again. Ten tricks linked in constant motion, her routine consisted of thirty seconds of circling, swinging, and seamless transitions from one bar to another. Apart from two strong straddle moves, her ankles looked like they had been tied together from the moment she mounted the bars to the moment her feet hit the mat.

Former Olympian gymnast Tim Daggett watched the high-quality routine, remarking on her release moves and handstand pirouette. As he anticipated her dismount, he said, "She has been landing so well at these national championships, giving nothing away."[50] And sure enough, she did it again, sticking the landing with her feet together. The cheering crowd knew it was great. So did the judges. She earned another gold.

After a long, hard month Dominique finally felt consistent. It hadn't been too long ago that she felt she couldn't stay on the beam. Now she performed with noticeable poise.

Tim Daggett noted her demeanor while he watched her on the balance beam. "I just mentioned the confidence she's exuding at these national championships. She better be confident right here, her major tumbling run: back handspring to three layouts."[51] Dominique travelled from one end of the beam to the other, mostly in the air. Just when the audience thought she would run out of beam, she lifted up in a confident end pose.

Even Nadia Comãneci, the world renowned gymnast, commented on Dominique's trademark difficult pass, saying, "It's amazing because she's not a short gymnast. She's pretty tall and how she can put together four [is something for me]."[52] Daggett concluded what the crowd was thinking: "This is incredible."[53]

Without so much as a bobble Dominique prepared for her dismount, two back handsprings, full-twisting double. Awesome Dawesome landed it and landed another gold.

Her powerful performance on the floor, the up-and-back tumbling pass, the enthusiasm of the crowd, her confidence and poise all exemplified her exceptional meet. By the end of the competition, Dominique had achieved something no other gymnast had done for twenty-five years. She "swept the board" by winning gold in each of the four individual events as well as the all-around.

In the most dramatic fashion, she became America's first African-American national gymnastics champion.[54]

The high-pressure, high-flying, highly competitive nature of gymnastics is hard even for the most practiced and most disciplined. A split-second break in concentration could easily result in a split-second slip on a routine the athlete could otherwise do in her sleep. And as every gymnast knew, a quick slip is the miniscule difference between standing on the podium or not. No wonder no other gymnast had swept the board in a quarter of a century.

Dominique had experienced a rare, blessed moment where it all came together. Unexpectedly the turning point hadn't been more practice, but had been some encouraging, heartfelt words of compassion.

In November, Dominique made a trip to Dortmund, Germany, to participate in the team competition of the

World Championships. She added a tricky release move to her bar routine, attacked her landings, entertained the crowds, and posted the third highest all-around score to help the American team win a silver medal. "She is just cleaner," said her coach of the improvements the veteran had made.[55]

What could inspire a top athlete to *improve* after so many years of grinding discipline and elite competition? Dominique could sum it up in fifteen words: "The love for what I was doing, passion for gymnastics, competing, and pleasing the crowd."[56]

It fueled her outstanding year in the sport. She was recognized as a finalist for the AAU Sullivan Award (recognizing top amateur athletes in the U.S.) and was named the Sportsperson of the Year by U.S.A. Gymnastics.

Her schedule still included seven or eight hours of training a day, but it didn't keep her from staying on the honor roll at Gaithersburg High. And the same girl who could beat the boys in fitness games with thirty-three pull-ups on the playground ("OK you can stop now," the teacher had to tell her) was voted prom queen.

On top of everything else, Dominique achieved another significant goal she'd been pursuing: she earned a college scholarship. She was invited to Stanford University to compete in gymnastics while pursuing her education.

The scholarship offer brought her to a major crossroads. Competition or education? Her decision came down to a matter of timing. The Olympics were two years away, and Dominique was in great shape to compete there. A lot could happen in two years, a lifetime for a 17-year-old gymnast.[57] Stanford would wait while she continued to pursue the part of her dream that wouldn't.

The memories of Dominique's unique successes would remain with her. So would the perspective that she gained during the disappointments. "I want [kids] to know that at the end of the day it's not always about 'Oh, I didn't win. I'm a loser,' " she said recently. "Even as adults we do that too if we fail at something, myself definitely included. [But] you've got to pick yourself up."[58]

Setting aside criticism would never be easy, but Dominique would try to simply do the best she could do. Remembering the wise words of Mrs. Norman would always help.

Chapter 6

Long Road to Magnificent Gold

"Sometimes you come out stronger."

Even as she focused on the upcoming Olympic competition, the nineteen-year-old widened her influence beyond the gym. Dominique was recognized for more than her tumbling technique with the Henry P. Iba Citizen Athlete Award which acknowledged an outstanding athlete who demonstrated good citizenship.

Until this year, Dominique was considered an "amateur" athlete, essentially meaning that she didn't draw a salary. By changing her status to that of a "professional," she effectively gained experience away from gymnastics (experience that, as it turned out, was invaluable). "[Becoming a professional] would entail getting endorsements, doing personal appearances, a lot of public speaking," she explained. "So it was more me being seen as a product and not just as an athlete anymore."[59]

Dominique had to alter her approach physically as well. Even as her goals were the same, her strategy had to change as she suffered injuries, including painful tendonitis, a stress fracture in her ankle,[60] and shoulder problems that developed as she compensated for a stress fracture in her wrist.[61]

The idea of holding back for injuries wasn't easy for the powerful gymnast. But with help from her coach, Dominique determined when she needed to work through the pain and when she needed to play it safe and let her body heal. With nearly a year until the Olympics, timing was critical. This year she had time to heal. Next year she wouldn't.

So Dominique skipped the World Championships early in the year as she focused on getting healthy. As it turned out, the time away paid off. She was able to compete in August in the U.S. Nationals—and compete well. She took first in bars and floor, third in beam, fourth in vault and all-around.

With an eye on the Olympics, she deferred the four-year-commitment to Stanford again, but eventually decided that she did better when she could concentrate on something other than gymnastics twenty-four hours a day. "I've decided to go to school because last year it was pretty much only gymnastics that I was concentrating on," she explained at the time. "It kind of got hard to have fun at what I was doing because it was only gymnastics. School would get my mind working on different things, so it helped me out a lot."[62]

Also to help her concentrate, Dominique posted motivational sayings that would help her focus. "I wake up with a burst of energy and optimism," she wrote on paper. Then, along with *D–3*, she put them around her room, on walls, lamps, mirrors, at home and on the road.[63]

"[Before the competition I would] just try to get my mind right while I was preparing. Because ninety percent of it when you're *at* the competition is mental. If you actually qualify for the meet, you're obviously physically good enough. You've been preparing physically. You can already do the routines. Your muscle has memory. And so it's really about getting your mind right."[64]

Going into the all-important Olympic year, Dominique felt the pressure to prove to everyone on the international scene that she was prepared physically and mentally. "I think everyone was kind of curious why I wasn't in Sabae [World Championships], and I want to show them I'm in really good shape if not better shape than I was before," she said.[65]

Dominique *was* in good shape. At the World trials, she took second in the all-around. At Nationals after a shaky start, she came back to score big on each event. She placed sixth in the all-around, and first on the vault, bars, beam and floor.[66]

At the Olympic trials, with her motivational sayings dotting the furniture around her hotel room, the nineteen-year-old performed well at the Fleet Center in Boston. Because of her accomplishments during the year, the coaches knew she was healthy and prepared. Consequently before she had even finished at the trials, she had pretty much sewn up a spot on the team.

But still the national champion of the beam didn't "water down" or take the easier road. She went for the most difficult dismount and scored a 9.825.

On June 30, Dominique finished first at the Olympic trials.

The United States hosted the Centennial Olympics in the summer of 1996. The top thirty-six gymnasts from all over the world came to Atlanta, Georgia, to compete.[67]

After thousands of hours of dedication and four long years since the last Olympics, the team competition came down to two nights when the athletes' actual performances would last a only few intense minutes.[68]

Traditionally the Russian and Romanian teams were the powerhouses, supported by the countries' established centralized programs. With its medal in Barcelona, the Soviet Union (now Russia) had won ten team gold medals in a row. Romania had decisively won the past two World Championships.[69]

The Americans didn't have the winning tradition and confident swagger of the Eastern Europeans. But renowned U.S. coach Béla Károlyi built an experienced, notable team to represent the country. Each team member had competed in at least one World Championship. And along with Dominique, three of them competed in the Barcelona Olympics.

Like her first Olympic Games, Dominique would compete for the team, but this time she would also compete in the individual events as well.

On July 20, 1996, the gymnasts got ready to enter the Georgia Dome to the deafening roar of the home crowd. "It was a plus," Dominique said about being in the U.S. "But at the same time it added a lot of pressure."[70] Of course Americans loved to cheer for their country, and the team wanted to give them something to cheer about.

"I nearly had a nervous breakdown before we walked into the arena," Dominique admitted.

7"I knew this was the start of it," Dominique explained, "and this was now thirteen years in the making. I nearly had a nervous breakdown because I knew what was at stake."

Amanda looked at her teammate. "I just said, 'You know what? We've done our job. We've worked hard for this. We've given everything we had. It's in God's hands. We go out there, we do our jobs, we have a blast. Whatever happens, happens."[71]

The competition began with the compulsory round where six members of each team performed identical routines on all four disciplines. The international panel of judges scored each routine based on execution (how well it was performed).[72] Essentially this first round put the team in a lead position or way behind without a chance to catch up.[73]

After the compulsories, the U.S. team was in second place behind the Russians. For the next round, or optionals, the gymnasts perform original routines (they have the *option* of performing more difficult maneuvers).[74]

In front of a crowd of more than 30,500 people,[75] every single gymnast on the team contributed to the close competition. Dominique, proficient in optionals, was the only team member to have all eight of her scores count toward the total.[76]

Throughout the night, the scores remained so close, the top three teams kept switching in the standings.[77] The cheers of the massive crowd grew as the Americans held up to the pressure of the strong Russians and Romanians.

Going into the last rotation of the team competition, the U.S. had built a lead, but it seemed like it could slip away. The U.S. still had the stunning chance to lock their place on the podium, but veteran Kerri Strug would have to land her vault almost perfectly on an injured ankle. The coaches, the crowd, the team didn't dare breathe—until Kerri landed it and effectively sealed the first U.S. team gold.

By the end of the night, the team knit together an accomplishment that would never be forgotten. With an African-American, a Romanian-American, and an Asian-American on the seven-member squad, the diverse backgrounds made it look more like the diverse country they represented than it ever did before. Dominique became the first black woman of any nationality to win an Olympic gold in gymnastics.

For the first time in forty-six years, a non-Eastern Bloc country won a world or Olympic title in gymnastics.[78] At the Centennial Olympic Games in front of a home crowd of more than 30,000 people (and a broadcasted crowd

John Gaps III/AP Images

Members of the Magnificent Seven wave to the crowd after being awarded their gold medals in the team competition at the 1996 Summer Olympic Games. From left are Amanda Borden, Dominique Dawes, Amy Chow, Jaycie Phelps, Dominique Moceanu, Kerri Strug, and Shannon Miller.

of more than 214 countries worldwide),[79] the United States Women's gymnastics team—later nicknamed the Magnificent Seven—stood at the top of the podium and from their necks hung gold.

Forty-eight hours after the dramatic team competition, the individual all-around competition began. Fractions of a point would decide this contest; a minor mistake would be the difference between the top of the leader board and the bottom.

On the first rotation, Dominique performed on the uneven bars. As the commentator watched her routine, he said, "What makes this young lady so exciting is her *big* gymnastics." And as if to prove his point, Dominique executed a huge release move that catapulted her body four feet over the highest bar. Her full-twisting double on the dismount gave her a super start and secured second place in a tight race that would last into the night.[80]

As she waited for her turn on the balance beam, Dominique concentrated on staying loose and focused. Finally she got her turn. Even with a five-inch growth spurt since Barcelona, she managed to fit in the impressive, long, acrobatic series that took her the length of the beam. The judges watched her difficult dismount and awarded her a 9.825. With it, she moved into gold medal position.[81]

As the athletes took up new positions for their third apparatus, the packed Georgia Dome was a pressure cooker. The American competitors were coming down off the summit of the unprecedented team success. With the expectant crowd inside, the incalculable international audience watching on TV, the President and First Lady clapping just yards away, the cameras filming just inches away, all of the gymnasts felt the strain. Tears of disappointment from many of the seasoned athletes only confirmed the extreme pressure that intensified as the night went on.

Dominique entered the third rotation, the floor exercise. Two nights before, she had pulled off the second highest optional score behind a Romanian. The crowd was behind her, knowing what this powerful tumbler could do on the mat. "I knew I was up," Dominique

Manny Millan/Sports Illustrated/Getty Images

Amazing leg strength gives Dominique the ability to get great height above the balance beam at the Olympics.

said. "I was just trying to clear my mind of that, but it is really hard when you are walking around the arena and everybody is cheering for you."

On the second tumbling pass, she felt her momentum carrying her toward the edge of the mat. In an effort to stay in bounds, she fell backward. Quickly gathering herself, she stood up and kept going, taking a deep breath before the last pass.[82]

Only after her last bow did the determined look she had maintained throughout the day dissolve into tears. She came off the floor and took a seat, disbelieving, dazed, devastated. She took a deep breath to "clear it out" in the words of her coach. When the score came up, the crowd booed its disapproval of the judgment, but Dominique didn't even look. She knew her chance for an all-around medal had disappeared.

"I don't think the all-around competition mattered more than team [competition], but it was just as high," said her coach Kelli Hill after the competition. "She knew this was her shot. She hung in for four years to go after it. It was a heartbreak."[83]

For some time Dominique struggled to get over the letdown and to make sense of the uncharacteristic routine. "I guess when it's for the team, I know I want to lead other people," she attempted. "And when I do it for myself . . ." she trailed off.[84]

But she would have to do just that—execute in Olympic competition when it was just for herself, not the team, because only a few short days later, the gymnasts

AF/AFP/Getty Images

Dominique performs her routine in the Olympic individual floor event on July 29, 1996. Dawes took the individual bronze medal in this event.

returned to the Georgia Dome. Specialists would compete for medals on each of the four individual disciplines.

Coach Kelli Hill took her protégé aside. "Dom, there's nothing you can do about [the slips in the past]," she told her. "It's going to hurt now and thirty years from now. That's just the way it is, and it's over with and we have to go on."[85]

And so she did. In a new red leotard adorned with bright white stars, Dominique stepped onto the same springboard floor that she had spent mountains of memories on already. With every high-flying, gravity-defying, straight-bodied, clean-lined, pointed-toe trick, Dominique gained momentum.

On the second pass, Dominique powered across the floor, felt herself complete it cleanly, and allowed a smile to light up her face. The thunderous crowd solidly behind her, Dominique's routine ended on beat and inspired a standing ovation.

The routine was the same one she had performed in the all-around competition, but the outcome, the score, the mood was different. Former Olympic medalist Tim Daggett commented, "That was awesome. Incredible routine. We're finally seeing all that Dominique Dawes has to offer."[86]

Relieved and happy to end her Olympic experience on this note, Dominique got a hug from Coach Hill and a beaming Béla Károlyi.[87]

By the end of the night, a hard-earned bronze medal hung around her neck. "I got a second chance,"[88]

Dominique waves to the crowd after being awarded the bronze medal at the women's individual event gymnastics finals of the Centennial Summer Olympic Games in Atlanta. By winning the bronze in the floor exercise finals, she became the first African-American ever to win an individual event medal in gymnastics.

Susan Ragan/AP Images

Dominique said at the time. And she made the most of the opportunity.

"You have to be ready to face setbacks and obstacles," she said later. Of course she trained to be perfect and not make a mistake, but it happened. She didn't *choose* to sit on the mat during the all-around but it happened. "I didn't like that at all," she admitted, "but sometimes you come out stronger. I want to inspire people of all ages to seek their opportunities and to never give up."[89]

As time rolled on and years passed, Dominique's perspective changed. Not only did the painful disappointment fade, but an appreciative recognition for the magnitude of the moment grew.

By winning the bronze in the floor exercise finals, she became the first African-American ever to win an individual event medal in gymnastics. A decade after the achievement, she reflected on her unique position. "Being there on that stage," she said, "and having young girls see a diverse team is what allows that sport to be seen as an opportunity for them.... They see someone who looks like them finding success."[90]

Dominique wanted to be a gymnast. She worked hard to achieve her dreams in the Olympics. With her hard work and accomplishments, she found herself a history maker, a pioneer, and an example. "It didn't hit me then. And to tell you the truth, it's probably still hitting me."[91]

Chapter 7

Audiences Fit for Rock Stars

"What I was feeling was a different story."

After the summer games, the United States delighted in Olympic fever, especially for the women's gymnastics teammates who so memorably took the gold medal. Their momentous accomplishment, their unforgettable nickname, their familiar faces captured everyone's attention.

The Magnificent Seven made appearances on talk shows, at the White House, and on a famous cereal box. "Better eat your Wheaties!" they said in unison on film. "We did!"[92]

Dominique had been a professional athlete for a year, but winning the Olympic medals in front of a vast worldwide audience created more opportunities to explore. Because people recognized Awesome Dawesome, they

Dominique holds a Wheaties cereal box that features members of the U.S Olympic women's gymnastics team.

wanted her to make an appearance, speak to an audience, perform a great trick, or sit for an interview.

For a couple of years, she retreated from the exacting competition of Nationals and Worlds, and instead competed in professional meets. In the new format she could exercise more creativity where the restrictions and requirements weren't so narrow and the pressure was less intense. Of course Dominique didn't hold back.

In the 1997 Women's Pro Championships, she did her floor routine to Aretha Franklin's "Respect" where she unleashed her up-and-back tumbling pass from one corner of the mat to the other and back again. In return she got the "respect" of judges who appreciated her amplitude that demonstrated she was giving her all.[93]

In the World Pro Championships the following year, the announcers were happy to see her. "Talk about a great athlete," they said. "She is a natural. She's very powerful, always taking a lot of risks."[94] Even after falling out of contention, she continued to perform the most difficult skills, including the most challenging beam dismount of the competition.[95]

She competed in the American Classic and the Goodwill Games, but like most of her teammates, she spent much of her time performing in a tour across the nation. As a group, the gymnastic champions toured thirty-three cities to perform for audiences of as many as twenty thousand. While the majority of spectators had seen gymnastics on TV, the tour gave fans the opportunity to see their favorite gymnasts in person.

"It was amazing," Dominique said of the experience. "We were on tour for nearly two years, and the fans treated us like rock stars."[96]

Most of her structured life had been spent training, practicing, and focusing in a closed gym. But with this

Richard Corkery/NY Daily News/Getty Images

During a temporary break from her gymnastic career Dominique participated in the Broadway show Grease and played Patty Simcox, the head cheerleader at Rydell High.

distinctive show, athletes had the unique chance to really grasp the impact they could have on a wide audience. For Dominique, the fact that she was inspiring others in turn inspired her.

Twenty-year-old Dominique also took the opportunity to be on a different kind of stage. She went nearly two hundred miles from Silver Spring to perform on Broadway in New York. The musical "Grease" needed a bouncy head cheerleader, and Dominique was their girl.

Dominique rehearsed long days for her run on Broadway. "It was interesting because I never really acted in school and didn't have the personality for it," she admitted. "I originally was terrified."[97]

Terrified especially when a former teammate from the national squad showed up to catch a show. In the audience was accomplished gymnast Shannon Miller, the one coaches used to pair up with Dominique as a roommate during international competitions because they were both quiet, serious, all about business. "I saw her and just froze," she said. "It was less than a second, but I was like, 'Shannon's here!'"[98]

During her stay in New York, Dominique realized the City wasn't for her. So when her stint on Broadway ended on New Year's Eve, Dominique was happy to go back home to Maryland. It suited her. "I am a very simple person," she explained. "I don't really need a lot of things going on. I like the quietness of Maryland. I love the diversity. If I want to get to a city, D.C. is right down the street, but I'm not *in* the city. If I want to get to the mountains or the beach, it's all within driving distance. And I love the four seasons."[99]

So she purchased a new place and settled in. She was home.

An audience could see that Dominique fearlessly conquered obstacles and challenges. What they couldn't see was that Dominique still struggled with mental gymnastics. "While everything seemed so perfect on the outside, what I was feeling was a different story," she explained. "The gymnast that people around the world saw on TV back in 1996 — a strong, confident, mature athlete — was not the same person I saw and felt from the inside. Despite having reached so many of my goals and having achieved what others would consider great success, I was struggling with a lifetime of self-esteem issues."[100]

Through sheer will and determination she could gut things out and pull off some serious accomplishments. But the uncertainty and disconnect between the outside and inside was still a challenge.

It was easy to see that Dominique's fortitude and perseverance served her well. Harder to recognize was that the ache of insecurity served a worthwhile purpose too. Dominique's own struggles cultivated a heartfelt empathy for those suffering a lack of self-esteem too. Although she didn't recognize it at the time, God had her on a path that would use Dominique's own suffering to offer compassion and inspiration to others. Moreover, the experience of helping others would help Dominique herself.

After the Olympics she explored all the opportunities outside of gymnastics that the sport had afforded her. It was invaluable training for her life after gymnastics. But that time hadn't come just yet.

Chapter 8

Back to the Mat

"I have this crazy idea."

After her stay in New York and the gymnastic tour, Dominique moved home and started school at College Park. (Stanford's unique curriculum meant hardly any of the credits she'd already earned would have transferred. Instead of essentially starting over, even with a scholarship, she continued with the University of Maryland.)

It was at school that Dominique considered making an unexpected turn in her life. "I had been in economics class daydreaming about making the Olympic team," she said. Could she dare try to make the daydream a reality?

She called her coach. "I have this *crazy* idea ...," Dominque told her. *Crazy* because Dominique had not worked out in over a year; *crazy* because the extreme

physical demands of competition favor younger athletes; *crazy* because Dominique was twenty-three which
is fresh only outside of gymnastics; *crazy* because since
1923 there have been only four female gymnasts to compete in three Olympic games much less medal.

"Part of me was hoping [coach] would say, 'Give it
up,'" Dominique admitted. "But she said, 'I want to see
you at practice tomorrow.'"[101] Dominique went to the
woman who knew her best. And together they decided
that with significant doses of *D-3*, the twenty-three-
year-old should go for it. But it would prove tougher than
ever.

"It was embarrassing," Dominique admitted when
she started. "An Olympic gold medalist who was not
able to do the basic tricks anymore. Even swinging on
the bars was hard because I had lost all the calluses on
my hands."[102]

Gymnastics hadn't changed and yet everything was
different—her perspective, training, body, mentality.
"I'd started gymnastics when I was six," she said, "but
it wasn't until I had to learn it all again that I realized,
'This is hard!' I gained a whole new respect for [it]."[103]

Dominique knew the amount of work it took to get
to the Olympics. And she knew she wasn't doing it.
"It was very difficult to stay in the sport with all these
young kids," she admitted." I was struggling. I went out
of town for work and told my coach, 'Don't worry, I'm
going to work out.' But I'd go to the gym and sit on the
mat talking to my friend. My coach would call and say,
'How's it going?' and I'd say, 'I'm getting there.'"[104] But

frankly to "get there" at the rate she was going, it would take her ten years.

"I think I was focusing way too much on, *I've passed my prime*, or, *What if I don't qualify?*"[105] Dominique acknowledged. The questions only slowed her down. Once she started taking *herself* seriously, she started really moving toward her goal.

"It wasn't until I did an interview and said I was training for the Olympics that I really started to take it seriously," she realized. "I wanted to make sure my actions were matching up. I started eating better, getting more sleep, going to the gym."[106] When she publically committed, she found her focus.

At training camp in June, Dominique showed how far she had come. Former Olympian Tim Daggett said at the time, "[It's] remarkable what she's trying to do in so little time in preparation, but her coach, Kelli Hill, says this young lady does better when she knows her back is up against the wall."[107]

Olympic coach Béla Károlyi, who had coached nine Olympic champions, liked what he saw too, calling Dominique the biggest surprise overall in a U.S. field of very good women gymnasts.[108]

At the 2000 Olympic trials, fourteen gymnasts battled for six spots on the team (plus two spots for alternates)—except that two of the girls were "locks," or in other words already selected based on their previous performances and reputations. So really there were *four* positions available in a competition where tenths of a point would determine who was competing in Sydney and who was watching it on TV.

Veterans who wanted to compete had to prove that they could hang with the younger kids. Shannon Miller (Dominique's accomplished teammate in Atlanta and roommate at several meets) put it this way: "Experience doesn't matter if you don't do what you need to do when the time is right."[109]

Dominique was not a lock. At the Fleet Center in Boston, she needed to bring it to every routine, every apparatus, every move.

Under the watchful eyes of many coaches including Károlyi, the gymnasts had to prove they could withstand the relentless pressure. After two days of competition, Károlyi would take the scores into a room, discuss strategies with the team of coaches, and make final determinations for the team.

In back-to-back performances, the athletes went through four rotations one night and then did it again a second night. The uneven bars gave Dominique the opportunity to display her huge release moves and difficult landing. One analyst noted, "At national championships, she performed so spectacularly on uneven bars, I actually saw Béla [Károlyi] giving high fives to everybody. He was impressed, and he says that Dawes provides big-time gymnastics."[110]

At these Olympic trials, Béla was equally animated. While Dominique performed her moves with precision and amplitude, the head coach watched intently, half standing out of his seat almost like he could help her stick her landing. She didn't need the help. When he saw her hit it, Károlyi stood and clapped as Dominique waved to the crowd.

Tim Daggett added his commentary: "Béla Károlyi loves her style, mostly on the uneven bars. He says it's a unique, big routine."[111]

At first Dominique was less than a point-and-a-half behind the leader. It put her in ninth position. After four rotations she had moved up two spots. She knew she was "on the bubble," not definitely going to the Olympics and not definitely staying home.

The Summer Games always delivered serious emotional and physical pressure, and Károlyi was looking for someone who was "capable of representing her country."[112] One commentator who watched the competition unfold remarked about Dominique's experience in representing the U.S. "She has been in this position before, the pressure, she knows what it's all about and she looked cool."[113]

Dominique, who launched her comeback mere months before, placed seventh overall and convinced judges, experts, decision makers, and coaches that she could help the American team.

She was going to Sydney. "I don't think I *deserved* to be on the team," she said. "I came here and wanted to *prove* I belonged. Just because I made it in '92 and in '96, that doesn't give me the right to think I belong in 2000."[114]

Dominique joined her Magnificent Seven teammate Amy Chow and a new crop of gymnasts to make up a talented team of women from ages sixteen to twenty-three. By making the team she also became a member of an exclusive club of women gymnasts that have competed at three Olympics.

"When I made the team, it was a proud moment," Dominique admitted.[115]

The pressure was far from over.

"Once you qualify and you make the team, you do not sit back and relax," Dominique explained. "The way gymnastics is set up, you might have qualified at the Olympic trials, [but] each and every day at practice between Olympic trials and the actual Olympic Games, is a competition. They can pull you from that team as quick as you qualified to get on that team. And so you know you have to be at the top of your game each and every day. They don't expect you to be perfect. They do expect to see some improvement, and not only physically with your skill level, but also psychologically. You need to make sure you're a good teammate, you're supporting one another, you're staying focused, you're not allowing external distractions and things get in your way. You're always dealing with pressures at the Olympic Games. There's the media. There are the fans. Family and friends even. If you can handle that well and you can show that you can handle that well, you're going to compete and represent your country. So they're going to keep you on the team. So the process, though it was like any other day in practice . . . there was a little more pressure because you knew your slot was not guaranteed.

But I think that's good, because it keeps people at the top of their game."[116]

Trial by fire means taking the heat of the high-pressure, do-or-die environment. Dominique grew up training for this, and, even after her time away, proved she thrived in the inferno.

Béla Károlyi, the Olympic coach known for his high expectations as much as his enthusiasm, appreciated what his veteran could do. When things got tough, he said, Dominique went in and nailed the routine. And then nailed another one.[117]

Realistically this team wasn't looking to repeat the team gold of Atlanta. But they did have a formidable goal in mind—make the podium and see their flag raised at the medal ceremony.

At the Games of the new millennium in Sydney, Australia, the United States joined teams from eleven other countries. Throughout the competition, Dominique showed the composure and skill of an experienced professional.

In the preliminary team qualifications, Dominique posted the Americans' lowest score on beam and the second highest on bars.[118] When all was said and done in the team finals, Dominique contributed to the team's final standing—fourth place. It was respectable, commendable, praiseworthy but off the podium.

Unusually however, the last chapter of the 2000 Olympics would be written ten years later.

During the competition, officials suspected that some gymnasts were defying the rules and were too young to

Reuters/Landov

Dominique performs her floor exercise during the women's team qualification in Gymnastics Artistic at the Sydney 2000 Olympic Games. She had to battle other younger competitors to get a spot on the team, but she worked hard and prevailed in order to participate in her third Olympics.

participate. Dominique refused to be distracted by the gossip. "As an athlete, when you're competing, you're not focused on the things you can't control," she explained. "Of course, I heard about the speculation of the athletes being underage. However, once I heard it, I quickly forgot about it. It was really something I didn't want to affect my performance in a negative way."[119]

After an extensive investigation that took years, it was determined that in 2000 one of the Chinese gymnasts was fourteen, two years younger than the rules allow. (The year Dominique was born, fourteen-year-old gymnasts, like Nadia Comãneci, were allowed to compete. In 1997 the minimum age requirement was changed to sixteen.)

The judgment brought up ethical questions of cheating and enforcement, winning at all costs vs. fair play. "The important issue is righting a wrong and hopefully prohibiting future Olympians from being underage," explained Dominique. "It's really about making sure every athlete is doing things the right way."[120]

Because Team China broke the rules, it was eliminated and stripped of its bronze medal. Every team with a lower score than the Chinese team, that played by the rules, moved up one spot in the standings. The U.S. team moved into the third place.

Dominique was excited to hear the news. "I got calls from reporters before receiving an email from the [Gymnastics International] Federation," she reported. "I also got a call from my coach, Kelli Hill, to congratulate me on the medal."[121]

On August 11, 2010, the International Olympic Committee awarded Dominique and her teammates the bronze.

"I could have never imagined getting another Olympic medal at thirty-three years old, so it's great to hear the news and that justice prevailed," said Dominique. "I'm thrilled that my teammates and I, ten years later, will finally be able to enjoy the medal we deserved."[122]

Ultimately the exciting new developments were tempered by a few regrets. "When I look at it, there are two things that bother me," Dominique acknowledged. "One, my teammates: This is their first medal and they didn't get to stand on the podium and have those medals put around our necks and have America watching on TV and be so proud of them. And number two, the Chinese gymnasts: The one thing that everyone's ignoring in this situation is that these gymnasts don't have a voice. They don't have a say. They're told that they're going to compete, and they're supposed to say they're a certain age, and it's sad. They are stripping these athletes, and they don't have a voice."[123]

In 2000 the U.S. team left Australia disappointed that they didn't reach their goal. "It was very difficult [at the time] not just for the gymnasts, but the coaches as well," Dominique explained. "When we got to Sydney, we didn't have gold medal on our minds, but we knew there was a possibility for us to get on the podium. It is good to know that ten years later, we did achieve the goal that we had set out to do."[124]

For Dominique, this last chapter of her gymnastics career meant she held the distinction of being the only American gymnast to win team medals in three Olympic Games.

Throughout her journey in gymnastics, Dominique earned an Olympic gold, three Olympic bronzes, three World Championships silver medals, one bronze World medal, seventeen gold National Championships medals, and two silver Nationals medals—twenty-seven hard-earned medals in all.

Much more than shiny ornaments, the awards commemorated a variety of memories and accomplishments. Even more they symbolized the triumph over big obstacles and the completion of even bigger dreams.

Chapter 9

Following Her Heart

"I love empowering and I love inspiring people."

After dedicating eighteen years of her life to her gymnastics journey, Dominique was ready to move on. "[The 2000] Olympics was for me and for my fans," she said. "It was a great way to end my career, but during those Games, I knew that I was done. I was losing the zest, the passion. I was very happy to hang up the leotard."[125]

She had wholeheartedly pursued a unique passion that included spinning on a beam, hurtling herself though space, and flipping in the air. It would be tough to replace.

For years her living situation, schedule, nutrition, and discipline had been arranged for the singular purpose of reaching her goals. And she had a long list of achievements to show for it. But with retirement all of this changed.

The gymnast was now a *former* gymnast. It wasn't just what she did. In many ways it was who she was. How would she define herself now? "I think once my career was over, it was a little bit of a shock to know that I was not going to be a gymnast for my whole life," Dominique admitted. "I was very thrilled I didn't have to wear a leotard anymore," she smiled, "but when I retired I had to do some soul searching."[126]

Dominique was staring into her future and wondering, *Now what?* Her gymnastics journey was over. But her life wasn't. What would her new journey look like?

Dominique needed something else she could do flips over. "It's not a need for competition or competing against someone else," she explained. "It's all about me pushing and challenging myself. I didn't want to push myself in just any arena. I wanted to be sure I would follow something I was passionate about. I did do Broadway for a little less than a year and realized I don't have a passion for it and, more importantly, I don't have a talent in it."[127]

Was everything she *did* have a talent for behind her? Were all of her achievements and inspiration behind her? She was only twenty-three. "I went into some dark moments," she revealed, "and really went into prayer for a number of years."[128] In searching for answers, she sought God's direction, listening to the One who knew her best, not just to those who meant well.

"My faith grew tremendously when I retired," she said. "I had done all I could in the sport and then I really

thought, 'What's next?' I didn't want to get caught up in the world, and that's when I really went to the Word."[129]

Her struggle eased as her relationship with God grew. And after a while the shadows became illuminated. "I realized I'm at my happiest when I'm coaching kids, when I'm motivating audiences, and planting a seed that's worth growing."[130]

Dominique came to see that all her years of practice and competition had given her a unique outlook on important life lessons. Overcoming disappointments, challenges, and obstacles concern *people* not just gymnasts. Persevering through doubt and finding a positive mindset in negative situations are lessons Dominique learned in the pursuit of championships, but translate to other life pursuits as well.

Maybe she could share some things she learned.

She knew a thing or two about setting goals and reaching them. She knew that the lessons she learned in the pressure cooker of competition could translate to school, work, and home. She knew that success and excellence is a long journey in gymnastics and also in life.

Maybe others could benefit from the struggles and lessons she learned during intense training.

Dominique took time and prayer to figure out what would give her significance. After searching and being still before the Lord, she came to realize she still wanted to inspire—only this time with her words, not her physical tricks.

"I like the thought of being able to inspire and empower people," she said. "And I've found the things I

learned throughout my career as an athlete can really help people."[131]

If she could encourage kids—and even adults—she would in turn feel encouraged herself. "It's always a thrill to rethink the experience [in gymnastics]—how it has helped shape me and how I can use it to be more inspired, more fulfilled, and more driven today."[132]

Slowly God revealed his sweet plan. Lift up others and find yourself lifted.

As Dominique settled into her new journey, she could hardly believe the irony herself. The one who grew up with a squeaky voice and shied away from speaking in the spotlight was choosing to do just that. "I didn't speak in class," she smiled, "and now [I wanted to be] a motivational speaker."[133]

"I think there's so much that people can relate to, such as the fear factor that I had to overcome time and time again," Dominique explained.[134] "When I look back on my gymnastics journey, it was eighteen years of hard work, of dedication and commitment, and focusing on the importance of proper nutrition. I look back at all those lessons to help educate and empower our youth and our next generation."[135]

Realizing her new inspired direction was only the first step. Next she had to *work* for it. "Let's just say I was not a natural," she laughed.[136]

It wasn't international competition, but there was plenty of pressure. Even if she no longer wrote *D–3* on her mirror with shaving cream, she was going to need as much determination, dedication, and desire as before.

"I think in any industry, it is competitive," Dominique explained. "There are a certain number of slots out there and opportunities out there. So you need to make sure that you're always on your toes, trying to get better."

So Dominique prepared herself first by getting grounded. "[I knew to] have principles in place before [stepping] out into competitive industry. You will be challenged; so stay true."[137]

Then she kept some things in mind. "You're not going to be successful in life, you're not going to accomplish great things in life, if you're doing it alone. You need good people around you. And also, going into everything with confidence, believing that you can and you will. Everything going on in your mind will control your body."[138]

Before her retirement from gymnastics, Dominique had taken courses from New York University and University of Maryland while training close to home. After determining her new direction, Dominique threw herself into studying her new craft. By 2002 she had earned a bachelor's in communications and broadcasting.[139] She interned at WNBC in New York in television broadcasting. And eventually she accepted work doing television commentary and reporting on special events.

Even now Dominique pursues her passion of encouraging and influencing people. Along with Dominique's work in broadcasting, she focuses on inspirational speaking about goal setting, leadership, and fitness. And she hosts one-day gymnastic clinics where she teaches the physical and mental tricks of her *first* passion.

"I realized I love motivating and I love empowering and I love inspiring people," she said. "I did that as an athlete for eighteen years, and I'm able to do that as a motivational speaker now as well as doing work on television."[140]

Whether on television, to singular groups, to kids, to gymnasts, there was a simple common thread for Dominique: "My goal is to have my stories really educate people and help them out in their lives."[141]

"I truly think it's my second calling and passion," she said. "After my speaking engagements, I feel so much more motivated and inspired."[142] When she retired, Dominique faltered without clear direction. Then God showed her the way.

As Dominique worked at the transitions in her life, she also took on something for pure pleasure—a puppy. Although allergic to dogs, she could tolerate Shih Tzus, sweet little hypoallergenic hair balls. Growing up, her family had three dogs, including a black and white Shih Tzu, and she always thought she would eventually get one of her own.

"I went into the pet store and there were black and white Shih Tzus there," she happily remembers, "and I could not remove myself from their little cages. And my cousin was looking at other dogs and asking, 'Aren't you going to look at those?' And I'm like, 'No,'" she laughed.

She had fallen in love. That day Dominique brought home Nelly. Three years later she got Marco. And then she gushes like a true mom, "They are just a joy."

Chapter 10

The Challenges That Need a Champion

"I want them to be empowered, educated on the importance of setting goals and working toward those goals."

With Dominique's faith, focus, and passion in place, she started using her new skills and education to help other people. Drawing from her own experiences, Dominique looked to inspire kids specifically about mental and physical fitness.

In the same way she kept positive people around her, Dominique knew that kids could use an encourager, another ally in facing their own pressures. After all, she knew something about pressure.

So coming alongside young people, Dominique threw her energies into tackling different challenges like she was running down the pommel horse.

Challenge #1: Self-Esteem

First she took on something that young people, including Dominique, had endured for a long time—a lack of self-esteem. "Because of my personal battles with low self-esteem from my childhood through young adulthood, aspiring to help build self-esteem in others became near and dear to my heart."[143]

Self-doubt didn't run away in the presence of a gold medal; it still made itself at home in the middle of all the accomplishments. Dominique knew how international titles and national adoration couldn't quite ease the pressure to be perfect and couldn't ease the disappointment when she couldn't be.

And then the words of Mrs. Norman come back: "We don't love you for your gymnastics, we love you for you, for who you are and the way you treat people."[144] Dominique's eventual freedom from the pressure to be perfect started here. The more she unloaded the weight of it, the more liberated she was to love others. She wanted others to feel that too.

In 2002, Dominique became the first spokeswoman for the Girl Scouts of America's "Uniquely Me!" self-esteem campaign for girls ages eight to fourteen. In partnership with the Girl Scouts Research Institute, the program aimed to reach 1.5 million girls in three years.

Dominique visited girls across the nation to talk about building self-confidence and a healthy self-image.[145] "Girls should know that everyone has to deal with self-esteem issues—even celebrities and top athletes," said

Awesome Dawesome herself. "I am proud to have the opportunity to reach out to girls through 'Uniquely Me!' and hope that we can empower girls to fulfill their dreams and aspirations."[146]

Partnering with the Girl Scouts and speaking to kids on her own, Dominique showed that it can get better. "As an adult I have come to understand that no matter what you do, you cannot please everyone, and that realization has helped me deal with my self-esteem issues."[147]

Kevin Wolf/AP Images for YMCA

Dominique encourages kids at the Washington Y to get 60 minutes of active play every day as part of the kickoff of YMCA's Healthy Kids Day™ in April, 2011.

If it's impossible to please everyone, it becomes easier to focus on who is important—those who love you, including the God of peace himself. With her foundation in faith growing all the time, Dominique realized that she was secure in the love of a faithful God. There was no need to be swayed by negative influences in an attempt to feel better about herself, she explained. And so she encourages kids: "You are never alone, so be true."[148]

For everyone, it's a lifetime journey learning to love God, others, *and* ourselves. And it's worth the pursuit. "Encouraging another to love herself is not an easy task," she said, "but it is a worthy task that is not only fulfilling for me but healthy for society. Imagine a world in which healthy self-esteem matters and you'll see a world in which we are blessed with kindness and compassion. Only when we love ourselves first are we capable of loving others."[149]

Challenge #2: Confidence Through Health and Well-Being

Continuing to inspire healthy self-assurance, Dominique took on another challenge in 2004. For two years, she served as president of the Women's Sports Federation, a charitable education organization dedicated to advancing the lives of girls and women through sports and physical activity.[150]

The organization was established in 1974 by tennis star Billie Jean King, and Dominique became the youngest serving president.

She already knew about the program since she served

as a mentor with the organization for nearly a decade. It only solidified what she already knew—that young women can combat self-esteem issues by getting healthy and getting active. "In speeches and in one-on-ones," she said, "I see how confident young women are when they're involved with sports. You see the difference."[151]

With funding and organized programs, the Women's Sports Federation encouraged young women by getting them "off the sofa and away from the computer" and getting them involved in physical activity. "We [weren't] trying to create athletes," Dominique said. "We just wanted them to have a fun activity that will do something for their health and well-being."[152]

Furthermore, from personal experience, Dominique knew that dedication to fitness contributed to dedication to other individual goals. It excited her to show kids how to recognize their potential and run with it.

"For young kids, I want them to be empowered and educated on the importance of getting out and setting goals and working toward those goals—either in athletics or the arts or academics—and understanding that their physical health and what they put into their bodies is truly important to helping them reach their full potential."[153]

Challenge #3: General Health and Well-Being

Even years after her last Olympics, Dominique was still getting recognized for the accomplishments of her first passion—gymnastics. So she continued to teach private lessons at her home gym and one-day clinics for competitive gymnasts. She emphasized fundamentals, goal setting, and mental toughness, skills they could take out on the mat and out into the world.

She also joined the advisory board of Sesame Workshop's "Healthy Habits for Life" program. And she made an appearance on *Sesame Street* to show furry, red Rosa (and millions of kids watching) how something fun and easy like frog jumps could keep a body healthy and strong.

And as cohost of Yahoo! News Weekend Edition she focused on fitness, sports, and wellness. "Getting the opportunity to cohost this show and talk about issues that are very important to me has been great,"[154] she enthused. "I'm considered an expert, and I am thrilled," she said, referring to her unique experience.

Dominique also supported organizations with missions that specifically promoted health and exercise for people with special needs. Because although she had accomplished physical wonders most people wisely never attempt, she saw her little brother battle serious impairment.

When Don Jr. was about three years old, he started showing signs of autism, a developmental disorder that affects the brain's normal development of social and communication skills. Not even ten herself, Dominique was unfamiliar with what autism really meant for her brother.

"I remember as a child wanting to *fix the problem* and not really knowing what the issue was," Dominique admitted. "I remember being home when he was a little older helping him write, trying to get him to pronounce words, and I remember thinking, 'Oh, he's just not try-ing hard enough.' Of course when I got older, I started recognizing that this is a serious disability and that he's not capable at the moment."[155]

At the time, the conventional wisdom was to "main-stream" children with autism by including them in regu-lar classes. Looking back she wondered if Don Jr. had had other opportunities or programs, how much more would he have flourished. "There are different paths you can have your kids go on today and they can learn so much more."[156]

So Dominique gladly assisted organizations that spe-cialized in programs for people with special needs. She supported Autism Speaks, a nonprofit organization that does research and provides information to families di-rectly affected by autism. She also became an honorary board member for the national nonprofit KEEN (Kids Enjoy Exercise Now). KEEN's mission is to foster self-esteem, confidence, skills, and talents through recre-ational opportunities for children and young adults with disabilities.

"I just truly believe in the work that they're doing, because obviously it's something that my brother could have benefited from when he was younger."[157]

The young achiever, who at first misunderstood her brother's disability as stubbornness, supported autism awareness by going to Washington, DC as a presence at the 2001 Power of One rally. How many other people similarly misunderstood autism? Hopefully less when she added her voice.

Through appearances, speeches, governing boards, and journalism, Dominique loved supporting and encouraging others on their journey for their best health. And she continued to tackle these challenges — self-esteem, health, fitness — that were separate but related, distinct but interwoven. After a while it became clear she couldn't physically be everywhere she wanted, couldn't talk to every person she wanted. So she came up with a new idea to reach a wider, more varied audience.

Dominique had been setting goals even before she was five feet tall. "My dream is to be on the 1992 Olympic team in Barcelona." Check. "I'd also like to stay in the sport and hopefully get a college scholarship." Check. "I'd like to go for the '96 [Olympics]." Check. In one interview she spelled out three lofty goals. She reached them all and more.

From her heaps of experience she could lend specific advice on setting objectives, facing pressure, and reaching lofty goals. While Dominique's goals and capabilities were unique to her, setting a foundation to reach them was more fundamental. If the goals involved physical fitness or mental health or something specific to school, everyone could benefit from the passion, planning, and perseverance that it takes to reach one's full potential.

And while she still spoke on the subject at appearances, she decided to reach a broader audience than before. As producer, writer, and speaker, Dominique created a CD called *Envision*. In it she considered how to set specific goals and then reach them, how to stay motivated, how to withstand peer pressure and setbacks, how to dwell on productive attitudes.

Those who heard her message might not be in the Olympics, but Dominique could tell them how to get to their *own* gold medal moment.

Right after gymnastics, Dominique felt her way through some dark months wondering what the rest of her life would look like. And the God who quietly led her to her first passion showed her where she could find her second one.

After prayer and introspection, Dominique landed in God's perfect plan for her. She knew how to dream big, and she understood that God had even brighter ideas in mind.

Dominique was excited about her future and how she could affect others. "My competitive career is over, and I am happy with that. I've done so much, from motivational speaking and coaching—I have [the] motivational CD out for young people. Now I am working with the media, and this is a thrill for me."[158] Her future is as bright as arena lights.

Her competitive career was over, but surprisingly enough her Olympic experience wasn't.

Chapter 11

What She Missed the First Three Times

"It gave me a better sense of what the Olympics are all about."

In the summer of 2008, Dominique packed up to go to her fourth Olympics. Only this time, she didn't pack a leotard; she packed a laptop. Instead of competing in the Games, she was reporting on them, as part of Yahoo Sports.

With her unusual amount of experience as an Olympic athlete, she had an insider's point of view. So with the eye of an expert, Dominique did editorial pieces, interviews with athletes, news about the day's events, and reports on the inside scoop about gymnastics.

Although she was the rare gymnast to compete in three Olympics, the Beijing Games were a first for Dominique. The first time she even thought about seeing anything other than the inside of a gym; the first time she stayed for a solid month; the first time she attended the supersized celebrations that bookended the Games.

The opening ceremonies involve huge displays of fireworks and flags to officially kick off the games. Teams from each country parade into a packed coliseum among fanfare, cheering, dancing, and eye-catching celebration.

Usually the day after the ceremonies, day two of the Olympics, the gymnastics competition begins. So instead of spending time and stamina at the celebration, the gymnasts stay in to rest and focus.

The athletes generally agreed with the coaches' decisions to skip the opening ceremonies and watched it on TV instead. "We would make light of it," Dominique smiled. The gymnasts would point to the crowd on the screen, saying, "Where would we be? Insert us there."[159]

July 2008 was the first time in four trips that Dominique saw the opening and closing ceremonies in person. From the stands she watched the flag-waving athletes and coaches march into the palpable energy of the buzzing arena. It wasn't long before she noticed that her entire perspective on the Olympics was transformed.

As a participant before, her focus was necessarily narrow. Her performance in the days of competition was the only thing that mattered. As a reporter, her focus had to expand. Beijing was the first time she recognized how big and far-reaching the Olympics really were.

"When I was able to go [to the Opening Ceremonies] and sit in the stands, I really felt what those athletes were going through," Dominique recalled. "I remember tearing up. It gave me a better sense of what the Olympics are all about."[160]

She finally comprehended how much greater the Olympics were than one star athlete or one outstanding team. Even though she herself participated in the Games, they had always felt more limited in a way. Because of her youth, because she didn't stay in the Olympic Village, because she was so focused on her own events, she had been separated from the other athletes—not just the ones from the U.S. but from all other countries.[161]

However, in Beijing, in the crowd of the opening ceremonies, Dominique glimpsed something else. "You realize it's more than just yourself," she said. "[Before, as an athlete] you really don't feel the big picture. Or at least I did not until I was sitting in the stands."[162]

"It was just a very touching moment for me, and it felt like it completed my Olympic journey."[163]

Without the pressure to compete for her country, Dominique was free to experience the Olympics and the country as much as possible. "So while I was in China, I tried different foods every single meal, explored the city, went to the Great Wall. And it was a great experience."[164]

Dominique's Olympic experience will continue with the XXX Olympiad in London, England. First she'll attend the gymnastic trials in June, a month before the opening ceremonies. And as anticipation for the Summer Games builds, she'll work with a team from FoxSports.com on inspiring stories about Olympic hopefuls, including a shot-putter, swimmer, sprinter, and gymnast.

In her current work, Dominique is still sometimes blessed to hear how she has affected someone else. Recently FoxSports.com sent Dominique to profile an African-American gymnast whose training will be tested by the pressure of the Olympic trials. "We kind of surprised her because I guess she told someone that I was her favorite athlete," she said with a laugh. "And it was funny, *I* was crying and *she* wasn't."

In July 2012 Dominique will watch firsthand how London welcomes athletes from all over the world. As a reporter, and as an Olympic enthusiast, she wouldn't miss a thing.

Chapter 12

When the White House Calls

"I was on board right away."

In the summer of 2010 Dominique heard from the White House. It wasn't the first time. About a year before, she had joined the nation's First Lady, Michelle Obama, in Washington, DC to visit high schools. As part of Women's History Month, they joined other athletes, actresses, and business women to speak to students about setting career goals.

This time the administration was looking for a long-term relationship. Could Dominique serve on the President's Council on Fitness, Sports, and Nutrition to promote health and well-being on a national level?

"The President had selected me to be on the President's Council but also had recommended me to be cochair," she said. "Once they told me what my role

Astrid Riecken/The Washington Post/Getty Images

Dominique, second from left, cochair of Presidents' Council on Fitness, speaks at a childhood obesity conference. She uses her experience and influence to encourage both youth and adults to live healthy, active lives.

would be and who my cochair would be [NFL quarter-back Drew Brees], I was on board right away."[165]

Originally created in 1956 by President Dwight D. Eisenhower, the Council has expanded its objectives: "to engage, educate and empower all Americans across the lifespan to adopt a healthy lifestyle that includes regular physical activity and good nutrition. With programs, information, and awareness, get all Americans to lead healthy active lives."[166]

Their mission was as difficult as sticking a blind landing off the top bar. Not only was Dominique on the team to help, she was first in line. "I knew I could commit to what they were asking for, and any focus on fitness, sports, and nutrition is right up my alley. This has been my focus since my 1996 Olympic win."[167]

Of course, considering her life's work, Dominique believed in the mission and knew there was a need. "One in three young people are considered overweight or obese. Type 2 diabetes is no longer called 'adult-onset diabetes' because so many kids have it."[168]

"Initially I just assumed people knew the proper amount of physical activity time or they knew what were healthy food choices," Dominique explained. "I [soon] realized that people are not privy to that knowledge. So [the Council] educates and engages families and makes sure they know what is a good amount of physical activity per day."[169]

Educating and supporting the entire country is a huge assignment. But with the federal government behind the project, the collaborations were wider than before. The Council partnered with city mayors, community leaders, churches, schools, and parents. They tackled underfunded physical education programs, hosted events with the high-profile first family, and set up motivational programs like the President's Active Lifestyle Award.[170] (The Presidential Active Lifestyle Award recognizes adults for thirty minutes of physical activity and kids for sixty minutes, five days a week for six weeks out of eight weeks.[171]

First Lady Michelle Obama, center, and Dominique Dawes, right, participate in a fitness event with military families on the South Lawn of the White House in Washington, DC, in May, 2011.

Dominique took this perfect opportunity to get *everyone* involved. "When I became the cochair of the President's Council," she said, "one of my main missions was to ensure that we were educating and empowering those with special needs as well, not just American citizens that are considered fully-functioning. So I brought in organizations like KEEN [Kids Enjoy Exercise Now] to the President's Council and the young kids that are part of that group have been able to meet the President and the First Lady and have also taken part in a number of the fitness clinics."[172]

"It means a lot to me," Dominique continued, "because my younger brother, when he was little, used to

Charles Dharapak/AP Images

President Barack Obama is pictured with Dominique, left, as he and first lady Michelle Obama get ready to watch a gymnastics demonstration on the South Lawn of the White House.

love basketball. He was really, really good at basketball. Many times kids with autism will have a gift, and that was truly his gift when he was really young. And I even remember playing the game H.O.R.S.E. with him when I was little. He beat me and I was like, 'I quit!' "[173]

Laughing at the memory of her tiny brother beating his big sister, Dominique went on, "I just remember being in awe of him (and clearly I was a sore loser). I just wish there was an organization back then for him where he could have been a part of a group of other individuals with similar disabilities and could have come and have fun and played sports and done physical activities."[174]

"The President is very passionate about ensuring that Americans are making smarter choices when it comes to physical activity and nutrition," Dominique admitted. "And I must say, the First Lady is so down-to-earth that when I first did an event to kick off my role as cochair, she was out wearing nice clothes yet jumping rope with me along with young kids at a DC school."[175]

Dominique, the student who looked forward to recess and held the pull-up record in the entire school, wasn't as fit as she was as a gymnast. "I am not a good example," she exaggerated. "A brisk walk with my two little Shih Tzus [doesn't count] because people are passing me as I stop." In other words, even former Olympians could move more.

Dominique knew firsthand the benefits of physical fitness and was excited to get others on board. "Just the other day I was on Facebook and tweeting and telling my followers to celebrate 'Let's Move,' and one lady wrote back to tell me how great the program is and how she lost sixty pounds just by following the PALA program. More and more stories have come in where people are saying these programs are making a difference."[176]

For Dominique, stories like that feel like magnificent gold.

Chapter 13

Building on the Foundation

"I don't have to wear a leotard to impact the world anymore."

The work that Dominique does now is a lot like breathing. She thrives off of it, breathing out encouragement to others and in turn breathing in fulfillment. Her flexible schedule suits her now where the days are different, the hours are later, the travel plans change, and the fluidity of life is far from the structured living of how she grew up.

Her schedule allows her to work on the President's Council, make appearances, find meaningful stories to report on, and now pursue a master's degree in business. Enrolled at George Washington University, the program provides plenty of foundational instruction, along with practical, hands-on business development. "I've already cried once in my financial accounting class," she smiled. She'll earn her degree in 2013.[177]

As if she had time for anything else, she wants to learn knitting (a good hobby for the road), has her favorite Bible studies, likes yoga and pilates, and keeps a good yard ("therapeutic") in the same house she bought after her role on Broadway.

She still sees her former coach, Kelli—although rarely at the gym. Better if they have dinner or go hiking. But "then I realized I'm terrified of every animal out there," Dominique laughed. "I jumped when I saw a squirrel."[178] After their long, goal-oriented journey in gymnastics ended, a friendship continues. Just maybe not on a hiking path.

Although Dominique retired from elite gymnastics when she was twenty-three, her connection to the sport remained.

Eight years after her last flip in competition, she and the rest of the Magnificent Seven were recognized for their historic golden victory and inducted into the U.S.A. Olympic Hall of Fame. "This is a very humbling experience," she said at the time. "It's amazing to think it's been [so many] years since that wonderful achievement."[179]

The following year she became a member of another elite group. Along with four worldwide stars, Dominique was inducted into the International Gymnastics Hall of Fame. Recognizing seventy-five legends from twenty different nations, Awesome Dawesome joined other impressive leaders in their sport, including the Olympic champion when Dominique was born, Nadia Comăneci who was inducted in 1993.[180]

The next year, Dominique was inducted into the Washington, DC Sports Hall of Fame, becoming only the third woman to receive the honor. "To be in such a class of honorees is great and humbling," she acknowledged. "I'm blessed that they were not only able to induct a young gymnast but willing to induct another woman."[181]

During her years of competition, she was so intensely focused to succeed, she simply put past accomplishments "in a stack." Now she could take time to reflect on them, appreciate them—and share what she'd learned.

Of course appreciating what she'd done didn't mean simply living in the past. "If you're just like, 'Hey, I won a gold medal and I have three Olympics under my belt and I broke down barriers,' and you do nothing else, it means nothing," she explained.[182]

So Dominique takes her historic accomplishments and moves forward. "It's definitely a humbling experience just knowing that I was able to empower an audience and inspire an audience not only through my athletic accomplishments, but even in the work that I do today. I think that's why I have continued with the motivational speaking and even the reporting that I do."[183]

Grateful to God, planted in faith, and motivated to affect others keeps Dominique bounding forward, hurdling over obstacles, and racing toward her goals. "[I'm humbled to make] hopefully, a positive impact on someone else's life—plant a seed to help them really accomplish their dreams and whatever their goals are or to see life in a different perspective."

"I don't have to wear a leotard to impact the world anymore," she said. "I can actually do it by sharing my Olympic journey and the joys I had in the sport and also by opening up about some personal struggles. And I can help a young person or help an adult realize more with their lives."[184]

Endnotes

1. Personal interview with author, 1/20/12.
2. Dominique Dawes interview with Matthew Jordan Smith, http://www.youtube.com/watch?v=vsyJkJhFjo0.
3. "Gymnast Dominique Dawes," Oprah Radio, 7/29/08, http://www.oprah.com/oprahradio/Gymnast-Dominique-Dawes.
4. http://www.troester.com/gym/MenuW.asp.
5. Personal interview with author, 1/20/12.
6. Dominique Dawes, "Love Yourself First," *Ebony*, 5/08, http://findarticles.com/p/articles/mi_m1077/is_7_63/ai_n25409469/; retrieved from http://www.dominiquedawes.com/.
7. Personal interview with author, 1/20/12.
8. Ibid.
9. "Magnificent 7 Documentary: Anything to Win," (parts 1–5), YouTube, http://www.youtube.com/watch?v=7Yenh NZSuKc&feature=related.
10. Dominique Dawes official website. "Success Is a Journey, Not a Destination," http://www.dominiquedawes.com/.
11. http://gymnasticsleotards4u.com/gymnast-dominique-dawes.aspx.
12. "Dominique Dawes—1992 Dodge Challenge Perfect 10—Floor Exercise," http://www.youtube.com/watch?v=Lwbegq1mG2Y.
13. "Dominique Dawes—1989 Konica Grand Prix Floor Exercise," http://www.youtube.com/watch?v=sPsmTuawp1Q&NR=1.
14. Ibid.

15. "Breaking Records, Breaking Barriers," http:// americanhistory.si.edu/sports/exhibit/olympians/dawes/ index.cfm.

16. http://gymnastics.about.com/od/famousgymnasts/p/ DominiqueDawes.htm.

17. Dominique Dawes—1992 Dodge Challenge Fluff and Balance Beam, http://www.youtube.com/ watch?v=ZEqOJ03g5Qk.

18. Mary Buckheit, "Catching Up with Dominique Dawes," ESPN, 2/22/08, http://sports.espn.go.com/espn/ blackhistory2008/columns/story?columnist=buckheit_ mary&page=dawes/080226.

19. "Dominique Dawes—1992 Dodge Challenge Fluff and Balance Beam," http://www.youtube.com/ watch?v=ZEqOJ03g5Qk.

20. "Magnificent 7 Documentary: Anything to Win," (parts 1–5), YouTube, http://www.youtube.com/watch?v=7Yenh NZSuKc&feature=related.

21. "Dominique Dawes—1992 Dodge Challenge Fluff and Balance Beam," http://www.youtube.com/ watch?v=ZEqOJ03g5Qk.

22. Personal interview with author, 1/20/12.

23. Ibid.

24. Ibid.

25. Mary Buckheit, "Catching Up with Dominique Dawes," ESPN, 2/22/08, http://sports.espn.go.com/espn/ blackhistory2008/columns/story?columnist=buckheit_ mary&page=dawes/080226.

26. Dominique Dawes interview with Matthew Jordan Smith, http://www.youtube.com/watch?v=vsyJkJhFjo0.

27. Stephen Kloosterman, "Former Olympic Gymnast Dominique Dawes Touts Tough Love," *The Holland Sentinel*, 4/29/10, http://www.hollandsentinel.com/feature/ x43878235/Dominique-Dawes-touts-tough-love.

28. Dominique Dawes interview with Matthew Jordan Smith, http://www.youtube.com/watch?v=vsyJkJhFjo0.

29. "Dominique Dawes—1992 Dodge Challenge Perfect 10—Floor Exercise," http://www.youtube.com/watch?v=Lwbegq1mG2Y.

30. "Dominique Dawes—1992 Dodge Challenge Fluff and Balance Beam," http://www.youtube.com/watch?v=ZEqOJ03g5Qk.

31. Mary Buckheit, "Catching Up with Dominique Dawes," ESPN, 2/22/08, http://sports.espn.go.com/espn/blackhistory2008/columns/story?columnist=buckheit_mary&page=dawes/080226.

32. http://en.wikipedia.org/wiki/Artistic_gymnastics.

33. http://www.dominiquedawes.com/.

34. Richard Huff, "Olympic Ratings Slip a Bit, but Viewership Still Eye-Popping," NYDailyNews.com, 8/2/96, http://articles.nydailynews.com/1996-08-02/entertainment/18023197_1_convention-coverage-star-trek-spinoffs-nbc.

35. Maryann Hudson, "A Balanced Personality: National Gymnastics Champion Dominique Dawes Does Not Allow Herself to Be Easily Ruffled," *LA Times*, 3/4/95, http://articles.latimes.com/1995-03-04/sports/sp-38695_1_dominique-dawes.

36. Dominique Dawes interview with Matthew Jordan Smith, http://www.youtube.com/watch?v=vsyJkJhFjo0.

37. Ibid.

38. Mary Buckheit, "Catching Up with Dominique Dawes," 2/22/08, ESPN, http://sports.espn.go.com/espn/blackhistory2008/columns/story?columnist=buckheit_mary&page=dawes/080226.

39. Dominique Dawes, "Love Yourself First," *Ebony*, 5/08, http://findarticles.com/p/articles/mi_m1077/is_7_63/ai_n25409469/; retrieved from http://www.dominiquedawes.com/.

40. http://en.wikipedia.org/wiki/1994_World_Artistic_Gymnastics_Championships.

41. 1994 Worlds Dominique Dawes BB AA, http://www.youtube.com/watch?v=sFHO8wze-ok&feature=related.

42. Barbara Polichetti, "Olympic Gymnast Dominique Dawes Has Found a New Voice as a Motivational Speaker," 3/13/09, http://www.projo.com/economy/BZ_SUMMIT_DAWES_SIDEBAR_03-13-09_UEDLPEN_v8.30aa007.html.

43. Dominique Dawes interview with Matthew Jordan Smith, http://www.youtube.com/watch?v=vsyJkJhFjo0.

44. http://www.dominiquedawes.com/.

45. Ibid.

46. Dominique Dawes interview with Matthew Jordan Smith, http://www.youtube.com/watch?v=vsyJkJhFjo0.

47. http://www.dominiquedawes.com/.

48. Dominique Dawes interview with Matthew Jordan Smith, http://www.youtube.com/watch?v=vsyJkJhFjo0.

49. "Dominique Dawes—1994 US Nationals EF Vault 2," http://www.youtube.com/watch?v=ZOIsQarcQXc&feature=related.

50. "Dominique Dawes—1994 US Nationals EF—Uneven Bars," http://www.youtube.com/watch?v=LEansbFt8wQ&NR=1.

51. "Dominique Dawes—1994 US Nationals EF—Balance Beam," http://www.youtube.com/watch?v=qIpwvPPIL3M&feature=related.

52. "Dominique Dawes—1994 Hilton Challenge Balance Beam," http://www.youtube.com/watch?v=fysbtR00PVg&NR=1.

53. "Dominique Dawes—1994 US Nationals AA (all-around) Balance Beam," http://www.youtube.com/watch?NR=1&v=NbGeyQyCTGc.

54. Maryann Hudson, "A Balanced Personality: National Gymnastics Champion Dominique Dawes Does Not Allow

Herself to Be Easily Ruffled," *LA Times*, 3/4/95, http://articles.latimes.com/1995-03-04/sports/sp-38695_1_dominique-dawes.

55. Ibid.

56. Claudia Hudson, "Sports Hero: Dominique Dawes," The My Hero Project, http://myhero.com/go/hero.asp?hero=Dominique_Dawes.

57. "Dominique Dawes—1994 US Nationals AA (all-around) Balance Beam," http://www.youtube.com/watch?NR=1&v=NbGeyQyCTGc.

58. Dan Greenberg, "Catching Up With Dawes," Ex-gymnast Dawes urges achievers to prize the journey, *The Gazette*, 2/27/08, http://ww2.gazette.net/stories/022708/damaspo210355_32361.shtml; retrieved from http://www.dominiquedawes.com/.

59. Tricia Whitaker, "Dominique Dawes One-on-One Interview," uploaded 3/1/11, http://www.youtube.com/watch?v=0JewxPUlISw&feature=related.

60. "Magnificent 7 Documentary: Anything to Win," (parts 1–5), YouTube, http://www.youtube.com/watch?v=7YenhNZSuKc&feature=related.

61. Christopher Clarey, "Gymnastics; Separate Missions for 2 Americans," *NY Times*, 4/19/96, http://www.nytimes.com/1996/04/19/sports/gymnastics-separate-missions-for-2-americans.html?ref=dominiquedawes.

62. "Dominique Dawes Interview—1995 Visa Challenge—Women," http://www.youtube.com/watch?v=qjm9ElPkPf4.

63. Christopher Clarey, "Atlanta: Day 9—Gymnastics; Team Gold for Dawes Was Only Part of Plan," *NY Times*, 7/28/96, http://www.nytimes.com/1996/07/28/sports/atlanta-day-9-gymnastics-team-gold-for-dawes-was-only-part-of-plan.html.

64. Personal interview with author, 1/20/12.

65. Christopher Clarey, "Gymnastics; Separate Missions for 2 Americans," *NY Times*, 4/19/96, http://www.nytimes.

com/1996/04/19/sports/gymnastics-separate-missions-for–2-americans.html?ref=dominiquedawes.

66. "Dominique Dawes — 1996 US Nationals AA Balance Beam," http://www.youtube.com/watch?v=gL_k9g-c2SI&feature=related.

67. http://www.gymnasticsresults.com/olympics/og1996wag.html.

68. "1996 Olympics — All-Around, part 1 ," http://www.youtube.com/results?search_query=gymnastics+olympics+AA+final+1996+part+01&aq=f.

69. Candus Thomson, "Dawes' Golden Gleam Hasn't Worn," *Baltimore Sun*, 8/3/08, http://articles.baltimoresun.com/2008–08–03/sports/0808020117_1_dominique-dawes-magnificent-seven-gold-medal; retrieved from http://www.dominiquedawes.com/.

70. "Magnificent 7 Documentary: Anything to Win," (parts 1–5), YouTube, http://www.youtube.com/watch?v=7YenhNZSuKc&feature=related.

71. "Magnificent 7 Documentary: Anything to Win," (parts 1–5), YouTube, http://www.youtube.com/watch?v=7YenhNZSuKc&feature=related.

72. "Magnificent 7 Documentary: Anything to Win," (parts 1–5), YouTube, http://www.youtube.com/watch?v=7YenhNZSuKc&feature=related.

73. "1996 Tour of Olympic Champions," [2 of 3], http://www.youtube.com/watch?NR=1&v=9pT7YTchRxI.

74. "Magnificent 7 Documentary: Anything to Win," (parts 1–5), YouTube, http://www.youtube.com/watch?v=7YenhNZSuKc&feature=related.

75. Christopher Clarey, "Olympics; Final Gymnastics Warm-Up Event: Grumbling," *NY Times*, 7/19/96, http://www.nytimes.com/1996/07/19/sports/olympics-final-gymnastics-warm-up-event-grumbling.html?ref=dominiquedawes.

76. http://en.wikipedia.org/wiki/Dominique_Dawes.

77. "Magnificent 7 Documentary: Anything to Win," (parts 1–5), YouTube, http://www.youtube.com/watch?v=7Yenh NZSuKc&feature=related.

78. Nancy Armour, "Mag 7 Reunites for Hall of Fame," *USA Today*, 6/17/08, http://www.usatoday.com/sports/olympics/2008–06–17–1800367342_x.htm.

79. "100 Years of Olympic Marketing," http://www.olympic.org/content/the-ioc/commissions/marketing/evolution-of-marketing/.

80. "1996 Olympics—All-Around part 1," http://www.youtube.com/results?search_query=gymnastics+olympics+AA+final+1996+part+01&aq=f.

81. Ibid.

82. Ibid.

83. Christopher Clarey, "Atlanta: Day 9—Gymnastics; Team Gold for Dawes Was Only Part of Plan," *NY Times*, 7/28/96, http://www.nytimes.com/1996/07/28/sports/atlanta-day–9-gymnastics-team-gold-for-dawes-was-only-part-of-plan.html.

84. Ibid.

85. Ibid.

86. "1996 Olympics Event Final Floor," http://www.youtube.com/watch?v=gru3czNBqc8.

87. Ibid.

88. Sarah Grossbart, "What Ever Happened to ... OLYMPIC GYMNASTS," *US Weekly*, 8/11/08, http://www.nytimes.com/2008/08/12/business/media/12adco.html?ref=sports; retrieved from http://www.dominiquedawes.com/.

89. Barbara Polichetti, "Olympic Gymnast Dominique Dawes Has Found a New Voice as a Motivational Speaker," 3/13/09, http://www.projo.com/economy/BZ_SUMMIT_DAWES_SIDEBAR_03–13–09_UEDLPEN_v8.30aa007.html.

90. Mary Buckheit, "Catching Up with Dominique Dawes," ESPN, 2/22/08, http://sports.espn.go.com/espn/ blackhistory2008/columns/story?columnist=buckheit_ mary&page=dawes/080226.

91. "Magnificent 7 Documentary: Anything to Win," (parts 1–5), YouTube, http://www.youtube.com/watch?v=7Yenh NZSuKc&feature=related.

92. "1996 Tour of Olympic Champions [2 of 3]," http://www. youtube.com/watch?NR=1&v=9pT7YTchRxI.

93. "Dominique Dawes—1997 Women's Professional Championships, Day 2 Floor Exercise," http://www. youtube.com/watch?v=mIWC2FFThQM&feature=related.

94. "Dominique Dawes—1998 World Professional Championships, Day 1 Vault 2," http://www.youtube.com/ watch?v=hh745MQ4gMW&feature=related.

95. "Dominique Dawes—1998 World Professional Championships, Day 2 Balance Beam," http://www. youtube.com/watch?v=32dqNEQzCZ8&feature=related.

96. "Memory Games," *Washington Post*, 7/27/08, http://www. washingtonpost.com/wp-srv/artsandliving/features/2008/ memory-games–072708/dawes.html; retrieved from http:// www.dominiquedawes.com/.

97. Dan Greenberg, "Catching Up With Dawes," Ex-gymnast Dawes urges achievers to prize the journey, *Gazette*, 2/27/08, http://ww2.gazette.net/stories/022708/ damaspo210355_32361.shtml; retrieved from http://www. dominiquedawes.com/.

98. Kimberly Wong, "Hopelessly Devoted," *SI*, 12/30/96, http://sportsillustrated.cnn.com/vault/article/magazine/ MAG1009289/index.htm.

99. Personal interview with author, 1/20/12.

100. Dominique Dawes, "Love Yourself First," *Ebony*, 5/08, http://findarticles.com/p/articles/mi_m1077/is_7_63/ai_ n25409469/; retrieved from http://www.dominiquedawes. com/.

101. "Memory Games," *Washington Post*, 7/27/08, http://www.washingtonpost.com/wp-srv/artsandliving/features/2008/memory-games-072708/dawes.html; retrieved from http://www.dominiquedawes.com/.

102. Ibid.

103. Ibid.

104. Ibid.

105. Ibid.

106. Ibid.

107. "Dominique Dawes — 2000 US Nationals Finals Uneven Bars," http://www.youtube.com/watch?v=f-XskdkskBE&feature=related.

108. Ibid.

109. "2000 US Gymnastics Olympic Trials Day 1 Part 1," http://www.youtube.com/watch?v=z8eK773r3mE&feature=related.

110. Ibid.

111. "Dominique Dawes Balance Beam – 2000 US Olympic Trials Day 2," http://www.youtube.com/watch?v=TOYH6PJHVzM&feature=related.

112. Selena Roberts, "Olympics: The Road to Sydney; Miller Out, but Dawes and Chow Make Team," *NY Times*, 8/21/2000, http://www.nytimes.com/2000/08/21/sports/olympics-the-road-to-sydney-miller-out-but-dawes-and-chow-make-team.html.

113. "Dominique Dawes – 2000 US Olympic Trials Day 2 Balance Beam," http://www.youtube.com/watch?v=TOYH6PJHVzM&feature=related.

114. Selena Roberts, "Olympics: The Road to Sydney; Miller Out, but Dawes and Chow Make Team," *NY Times*, 8/21/2000, http://www.nytimes.com/2000/08/21/sports/olympics-the-road-to-sydney-miller-out-but-dawes-and-chow-make-team.html.

115. "Memory Games," *Washington Post*, 7/27/08, http://www.washingtonpost.com/wp-srv/artsandliving/features/2008/

memory-games–072708/dawes.html; retrieved from http://
www.dominiquedawes.com/.

116. Tricia Whitaker, "Dominique Dawes One on One Interview,"
uploaded 3/1/11, http://www.youtube.com/watch?v=0Jewx
PUlISw&feature=related.

117. "Dominique Dawes—2000 Olympics Team Prelims Balance
Beam," http://www.youtube.com/watch?v=GK6sCwXsQY
U&feature=related.

118. http://www.gymnasticsresults.com/olympics/2000/
wagqualteams.html.

119. Maggie Hendricks, "Ten Years Later, Bronze 'Special' for
U.S. Gymnast Dominique Dawes," Yahoo Sports, 4/29/10,
http://sports.yahoo.com/olympics/blog/fourth_place_
medal/post/Ten-years-later-bronze-special-for-U-S-
gymna?urn=oly–237736.

120. Nancy Armour, "Gym Officials: China's 2008 Gold
Medalists of Age," *USA Today*, 10/1/2008, http://www.
usatoday.com/sports/olympics/2008–10–01–635786566_x.
htm.

121. Maggie Hendricks, "Ten Years Later, Bronze 'Special' for
U.S. Gymnast Dominique Dawes," Yahoo Sports, 4/29/10,
http://sports.yahoo.com/olympics/blog/fourth_place_
medal/post/Ten-years-later-bronze-special-for-U-S-
gymna?urn=oly–237736.

122. Juliet Macur, "China Stripped of Gymnastics Medal," *NY
Times*, 4/28/10, http://www.nytimes.com/2010/04/29/
sports/olympics/29gymnast.html?ref=dominiquedawes.

123. Maggie Hendricks, "Ten Years Later, Bronze 'Special' for
U.S. Gymnast Dominique Dawes," Yahoo Sports, 4/29/10,
http://sports.yahoo.com/olympics/blog/fourth_place_
medal/post/Ten-years-later-bronze-special-for-U-S-
gymna?urn=oly–237736.

124. Ibid.

125. "Memory Games," *Washington Post*, 7/27/08, http://www.
washingtonpost.com/wp-srv/artsandliving/features/2008/

memory-games–072708/dawes.html; retrieved from http://
www.dominiquedawes.com/.

126. "Olympian Dominique Dawes Fights Childhood Obesity on
President's Council," myfoxdc, 6/25/10, http://www.
myfoxdc.com/dpp/mornings/olympian-dominique-dawes-
fights-chilldhood-obesity-on-presidents-council–062510.

127. Jeffrey Marcus, "Again in Front of the Camera," *NY Times*,
8/1/09, http://www.nytimes.com/2009/08/02/
sports/02seconds.html?ref=dominiquedawes.

128. "Olympian Dominique Dawes Fights Childhood Obesity on
President's Council," myfoxdc, 6/25/10, http://www.
myfoxdc.com/dpp/mornings/olympian-dominique-dawes-
fights-chilldhood-obesity-on-presidents-council–062510.

129. Tricia Whitaker, "Dominique Dawes One on One Interview,"
uploaded 3/1/11, http://www.youtube.com/watch?v=0Jewx
PUlISw&feature=related.

130. "Olympian Dominique Dawes Fights Childhood Obesity on
President's Council," myfoxdc, 6/25/10, http://www.
myfoxdc.com/dpp/mornings/olympian-dominique-dawes-
fights-chilldhood-obesity-on-presidents-council–062510.

131. Barbara Polichetti, "Olympic Gymnast Dominique Dawes
Has Found a New Voice as a Motivational Speaker,"
3/13/09, http://www.projo.com/economy/BZ_SUMMIT_
DAWES_SIDEBAR_03–13–09_UEDLPEN_v8.30aa007.
html.

132. "Memory Games," *Washington Post*, 7/27/08, http://www.
washingtonpost.com/wp-srv/artsandliving/features/2008/
memory-games–072708/dawes.html; retrieved from http://
www.dominiquedawes.com/.

133. "Gymnast Dominique Dawes," Oprah Radio, 7/29/08,
http://www.oprah.com/oprahradio/Gymnast-Dominique-
Dawes.

134. Barbara Polichetti, "Olympic Gymnast Dominique Dawes
Has Found a New Voice as a Motivational Speaker,"
3/13/09, http://www.projo.com/economy/BZ_SUMMIT_

DAWES_SIDEBAR_03–13–09_UEDLPEN_v8.30aa007.
html

135. "Olympian Dominique Dawes Fights Childhood Obesity on President's Council," myfoxdc, 6/25/10, http://www.myfoxdc.com/dpp/mornings/olympian-dominique-dawes-fights-chilldhood-obesity-on-presidents-council–062510.

136. Barbara Polichetti, "Olympic Gymnast Dominique Dawes Has Found a New Voice as a Motivational Speaker," 3/13/09, http://www.projo.com/economy/BZ_SUMMIT_DAWES_SIDEBAR_03–13–09_UEDLPEN_v8.30aa007.html.

137. Tricia Whitaker, "Dominique Dawes One on One Interview," uploaded 3/1/11, http://www.youtube.com/watch?v=0Jewx PUlISw&feature=related.

138. Jeffrey Marcus, "Again in Front of the Camera," *NY Times*, 8/1/09, http://www.nytimes.com/2009/08/02/sports/02seconds.html?ref=dominiquedawes.

139. Frank Litsky, "Ex-Gymnast's Next Routine Is Getting Girls Off Couch," *NY Times*, 5/21/04, http://www.nytimes.com/2004/05/21/sports/olympics-ex-gymnast-s-next-routine-is-getting-girls-off-couch.html.

140. Jeffrey Marcus, "Again in Front of the Camera," *NY Times*, 8/1/09, http://www.nytimes.com/2009/08/02/sports/02seconds.html?ref=dominiquedawes.

141. Ibid.

142. Melissa Jacobs, "Let's Move with Dominique Dawes," 2/14/11, http://espn.go.com/espnw/features-profiles/6120493/melissa-jacobs-move-dominique-dawes.

143. Dominique Dawes, "Love Yourself First," *Ebony*, 5/08, http://findarticles.com/p/articles/mi_m1077/is_7_63/ai_n25409469/; retrieved from http://www.dominiquedawes.com/.

144. Dominique Dawes interview with Matthew Jordan Smith, http://www.youtube.com/watch?v=vsyJkJhFjo0.

Endnotes

145. *"Olympic Champion Dominique Dawes Teams Up With Girl Scouts & Unilever To Empower Girls Through Progressive New Self-Esteem Program,"* Marketwire, 9/02, http://findarticles. com/p/articles/mi_pwwi/is_20050229/ai_mark03046497/.

146. Ibid.

147. Dominique Dawes, "Love Yourself First," *Ebony*, 5/08, http://findarticles.com/p/articles/mi_m1077/is_7_63/ai_ n25409469/; retrieved from http://www.dominiquedawes. com/.

148. Tricia Whitaker, "Dominique Dawes One on One Interview," uploaded 3/1/11, http://www.youtube.com/watch?v=0Jewx PUlISw&feature=related.

149. Dominique Dawes, "Love Yourself First," *Ebony*, 5/08, http://findarticles.com/p/articles/mi_m1077/is_7_63/ai_ n25409469/; retrieved from http://www.dominiquedawes. com/.

150. Claudia Hudson, "Sports Hero: Dominique Dawes," The My Hero Project, http://myhero.com/go/hero. asp?hero=Dominique_Dawes.

151. Frank Litsky, "Ex-Gymnast's Next Routine Is Getting Girls Off Couch," *NY Times*, 5/21/04, http://www.nytimes. com/2004/05/21/sports/olympics-ex-gymnast-s-next- routine-is-getting-girls-off-couch.html.

152. Ibid.

153. Candus Thomson, "Q&A with Olympian Dominique Dawes on Obama's Fitness Council," *Baltimore Sun*, 6/30/10, http://articles.baltimoresun.com/2010–06–30/health/ bal-dominique-dawes–0630_1_fitness-olympian-dominique- dawes-gymnastics/2.

154. Melissa Jacobs, "Let's Move with Dominique Dawes," 2/14/11, http://espn.go.com/espnw/features- profiles/6120493/melissa-jacobs-move-dominique-dawes.

155. Personal interview with author, 1/20/12.

156. Ibid.

157. Ibid.

158. "Gymnast Dominique Dawes," Oprah Radio, 7/29/08, http://www.oprah.com/oprahradio/Gymnast-Dominique-Dawes.

159. Personal interview with author, 1/20/12.

160. Ibid.

161. Ibid.

162. Ibid.

163. Ibid.

164. Ibid.

165. Melissa Jacobs, "Let's Move with Dominique Dawes," 2/14/11, http://espn.go.com/espnw/features-profiles/6120493/melissa-jacobs-move-dominique-dawes.

166. President's Council on Fitness, Sports and Nutrition, http://www.fitness.gov/about-us/who-we-are/co-chairs/dominique-dawes/.

167. Melissa Jacobs, "Let's Move with Dominique Dawes," 2/14/11, http://espn.go.com/espnw/features-profiles/6120493/melissa-jacobs-move-dominique-dawes.

168. "Dominique Dawes Promotes Exercise to Fight Childhood Obesity," *Washington Post*, 3/15/11, http://www.washingtonpost.com/wp-dyn/content/video/2011/03/15/VI2011031504249.html.

169. Raval Davis, "5 Questions for Dominique Dawes on 'Get Moving' Challenge," *Essence*, 7/11/11, http://www.essence.com/2011/07/11/5-questions-for-dominique-dawes-on-get-moving-challenge/.

170. "Olympian Dominique Dawes Fights Childhood Obesity on President's Council," myfoxdc, 6/25/10, http://www.myfoxdc.com/dpp/mornings/olympian-dominique-dawes-fights-chilldhood-obesity-on-presidents-council-062510.

171. Raval Davis, "5 Questions for Dominique Dawes on 'Get Moving' Challenge," *Essence*, 7/11/11, http://www.essence.

com/2011/07/11/5-questions-for-dominique-dawes-on-get-moving-challenge/.

172. Personal interview with author, 1/20/12.

173. Ibid.

174. Ibid.

175. Melissa Jacobs, "Let's Move with Dominique Dawes," 2/14/11, http://espn.go.com/espnw/features-profiles/6120493/melissa-jacobs-move-dominique-dawes.

176. Ibid.

177. Personal interview with author, 1/20/12.

178. Ibid.

179. "Samuelson, 'Magnificent Seven' chosen for US Olympic Hall," *USA Today*, 4/15/08, http://www.usatoday.com/sports/olympics/2008-04-15-463220745_x.htm.

180. http://www.ighof.com/.

181. Tamika Smith and Marty Chase, "Olympic Gold Medalist Dominique Dawes Inducted into D.C. Sports Hall of Fame," *Silver Spring Patch*, 3/22/11, http://silverspring.patch.com/articles/olympic-gold-medalist-dominique-dawes-inducted-into-dc-sports-hall-of-fame.

182. Mary Buckheit, "Catching Up with Dominique Dawes," ESPN, 2/22/08, http://sports.espn.go.com/espn/blackhistory2008/columns/story?columnist=buckheit_mary&page=dawes/080226.

183. Tamika Smith and Marty Chase, "Olympic Gold Medalist Dominique Dawes Inducted into D.C. Sports Hall of Fame," *Silver Spring Patch*, 3/22/11, http://silverspring.patch.com/articles/olympic-gold-medalist-dominique-dawes-inducted-into-dc-sports-hall-of-fame.

184. "Gymnast Dominique Dawes," Oprah Radio, 7/29/08, http://www.oprah.com/oprahradio/Gymnast-Dominique-Dawes.

Defender of Faith:
The Mike Fisher Story

Kim Washburn

Mike Fisher knows the true meaning of a power play.

As a veteran of the National Hockey League, Mike Fisher has a lot to be proud of. He plays for the Nashville Predators, was an alternate captain for the Ottawa Senators, competed in the Stanley Cup finals, and has been nominated for the Selke Trophy as the best defensive forward in the league. But it's not just his guts, grit, and talent that have brought him success. His power comes from the top—he puts his faith in Christ first and has demonstrated his love for God both on and off the ice.

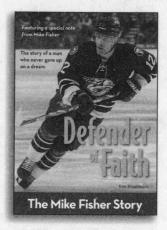

Available in stores and online!

Breaking Through By Grace: The Bono Story

Kim Washburn

When love walks in the room ...

Awards, fame, wealth ... Bono has it all. But the biggest rock star in the world has something more important, something that has guided every step of his success: faith in God. From growing up in Ireland during deadly times to performing on the largest stages in the world, Bono's beliefs have kept him grounded and focused on what truly matters. Whether

using his voice to captivate an audience or to fight for justice and healing in Africa, Bono is a champion of the lost and a hero to those who long for harmony.

We want to hear from you. Please send your comments about this book to us in care of zreview@zondervan.com. Thank you.